HARUNU'L-RASHID AND CHARLES THE GREAT

AMS PRESS
NEW YORK

HARUNU'L-RASHID AND CHARLES THE GREAT

F. W. BUCKLER, M.A.
Sometime Scholar of Trinity Hall and Allen Scholar
in the University of Cambridge; Professor of Church History
in the Graduate School of Theology, Oberlin College.

THE MEDIAEVAL ACADEMY OF AMERICA
CAMBRIDGE, MASSACHUSETTS
1931

Library of Congress Cataloging in Publication Data

Buckler, Francis William, 1891-
    Harunu'l-Rashid and Charles the Great.

    Reprint of the 1931 ed. published by the Mediaeval Academy of America, Cambridge, Mass., which was issued as no. 2 of the Monographs of the Mediaeval Academy of America.
    Bibliography: p.
    1. Islamic Empire—Foreign relations—France.
2. France—Foreign relations—Islamic Empire.
3. Hārūn al-Rashīd, caliph. 763 (ca.)-809.
4. Charlemagne, 742-814. I. Title. II. Series: Mediaeval Academy of America. Monographs; no. 2.
DS63.2.F8B8   1978   327.44'017'671   75-41041
ISBN 0-404-14761-5

Reprinted from an original in the collections of the Newark Public Library

From the edition of 1931, Cambridge, Mass.
First AMS edition published in 1978
Manufactured in the United States of America

AMS PRESS INC.
NEW YORK, N.Y.

PREFACE

AS far as I have been able to discover, the diplomatic relations between the 'Abbāsid and Carolingian houses have never been treated in English within the compass of a single essay. Certain aspects, as for instance the so-called Frankish Protectorate, have received considerable attention, but their treatment has always been in isolation from the political situation prevailing in Christendom or Islām, and but scant attention has been paid to the affairs of Spain. In addition, the significance of the gifts of the Caliphs to the Frankish kings and the diplomatic etiquette observed have been completely ignored.

In my own work in the political theory of Oriental Despotism, I was confronted with the place of the robe of honour in the ceremonial of commendation in the East, and the idea of applying the theory to the interpretation of Charles the Great's relations with Hārūnu'l-Rashīd appeared to be a fruitful one. In 1925 my attention was drawn to the relics of the *pallium* of Saint Cuthbert and the *kalima* woven into the purple robe. In a description of the relics, published in *Archaeologia Aeliana*, I gave a summary of the theory as a possible solution of the presence of a Muslim robe on the body of a Christian saint, but, within the limits prescribed, adequate treatment was impossible.

In the following essay, this theory has been developed and the results compared with the conclusions of Barthold, Vasiliev, and others, and I submit that in the light of the Umayyad and 'Abbāsid feud there is nothing inherently improbable either in the negotiations or in the form they took, particularly if the suggestion to Pippin came either from discontented Spanish *amīrs* or from Alexandria or from both. The fundamental condition to be borne in mind is that the approach made by Pippin, and later by Charles, to the Khalīfah placed them both in the status of petitioners, while the political framework underlying the negotiations was primarily Muslim. Hence, it follows that the whole chapter lies within the realm of Muslim rather than Christian history. In that light the grant of a 'protectorate' or *wilāyat* over the Holy Places is admissible; but it is to be assumed that it was as a vassal, not as an equal of the Khalīfah, that Charles received it. Similarly, too, the grant of authority over the 'Abbāsid party in Spain falls into the same category. Western historians and diplomatists have been far too prone to read into Oriental and mediaeval history the usages of their own diplomatic code, and, with the exception of Sir Thomas Roe's difficulties at the court of Jahāngīr, there are few examples more striking in the relations between the East and the West than this episode, whose dramatic irony culminates in the Pope's doing homage to the accredited deputy of the Successor of the Prophet of God!

I have used the system of transliteration approved by the Royal Asiatic Society except in the case of the summary of Barthold's essay, where I have followed his method. The editorial details conform with the rules laid down by the Academy for *Speculum* with one exception. In order to facilitate reference to the bibliography and to make the footnotes less cumbrous, I have used the name of the author followed by the number assigned to the work in the bibliography, where the title and all necessary details can be found.

I desire gratefully to acknowledge the help and suggestions I have received from many sources, particularly Professor R. A. Nicholson, who has very kindly checked the Arabic portions of the work; Mr G. W. Robinson, who read the whole of the manuscript; Mr B. J. Milovsoroff, to whom I owe my ability to use the works of Barthold and Vasiliev; Professor A. A. Vasiliev, for constant help and advice; the Committee of Productive Work, Oberlin College, which made a grant to cover the preliminary expenses of publication; the Mediaeval Academy of America, particularly Mr John Marshall and the Editorial Board, who have enabled this essay to be published, and Mrs C. J. Ormsby, Secretary to the Graduate School of Theology, for typing the whole essay. I desire too to thank the Editor of *Archaeologia Aeliana* for permission to reprint portions of 'The *Pallium* of Saint Cuthbert.'

I conclude with a note of regret and homage in recording the deaths of two European scholars to whom this essay owes so much: my old friend, Sir Thomas Arnold, who died on June the 9th last, and W. W. Barthold in September last.

F. W. BUCKLER

OBERLIN, OHIO,
JANUARY, 1931

CONTENTS

I. 'Abdu'l-Raḥmān and the Franks 3
II. Franco-'Abbāsid Relations under Hārūnu'l-Rashīd . . 17
III. The Status of Charles the Great 32

APPENDICES

I. 'Charles the Great and Harun ar-Rashid,' by W. W. Barthold 43
II. The Chronology of Cosmas, Patriarch of Alexandria . . 48
III. *Propter Elephantem Bestiam* 51
IV. An extract from 'The *Pallium* of Saint Cuthbert' . . . 53

BIBLIOGRAPHY 57

HARUNU'L-RASHID AND CHARLES THE GREAT

I

'ABDU'L-RAHMAN AND THE FRANKS

THE diplomatic relations of Pippin and Charles the Great with the Muslim world do not seem to have been collected in a single study in English, but appear only as scattered and unrelated incidents in the period 751 to 813 A.D. Any element of continuity or considered policy has consequently been obscured, though Felix Dahn and Edward Freeman appear to have realized that they probably formed an organic whole with the Franco-Byzantine relations. In this century, however, Barthold[1] has given a rude shock to any idea of Franco-'Abbāsid relations by his drastic rejection of the validity of Frankish authorities on the ground that they are not corroborated by any Muslim sources. Further, he maintained that he could find no matter of sufficient importance in Frankish affairs to account for 'Abbāsid interest. More recently, the topic has acquired a renewed interest from certain criticisms of Bréhier's paper on the Frankish Protectorate in the Holy Land made by Professor Halphen and followed up more elaborately in the surveys of Kleinclausz and Professor E. Joranson.[2]

It must be admitted at the outset and borne constantly in mind that any final decision is difficult, owing to the unsatisfactory state of the surviving records, both Christian and Muslim; but despite the fragmentary nature of these authorities, there do appear certain well marked developments which seem to arise from the combined consequences of the 'Abbāsid and Carolingian revolutions. The solution of the problem appears to lie within the realm of Muslim politics, which determined both the form of the settlement and the formalities

[1] As Barthold's article is somewhat inaccessible to English readers, a summary is given in Appendix I. For Freeman's views, see no. 92, pp. 256-260.
[2] The controversial literature in this subject is conveniently summarized in the following places: Joranson, no. 107, p. 241, nn. 1-2; Kleinclausz, no. 109, pp. 211, nn. 1-2, 212, n. 1, 227-232; Bréhier, no. 60, a reply to the above articles. It may be permitted to add to the above references my article 'The *Pallium* of Saint Cuthbert' (no. 72). The theory of Eastern kingship on which this interpretation is based has been summarized by me in a paper entitled 'The Oriental Despot' (no. 67).

of the transactions. Examined from the 'Abbāsid point of view, the Frankish records reveal a political situation in the Muslim world which would provide the 'Abbāsids with a strong motive for intervening in the affairs of the West and for seeking to make use of the military and naval resources of the Franks. In addition, the results of the policy reveal, when considered in the light of Perso-Muslim political theory, a development of 'Abbāsid pretensions which culminated in a claim to overlordship over Spain through the medium of Pippin and Charles the Great.

In that setting, it is at least conceivable that the episode of the grant of authority over Jerusalem and the Holy Places is historical, for the details recorded by the *Annales Regni Francorum* and Einhard, not to mention the curious account of the anonymous Monk of Saint Gall, are quite consistent with the technique of Perso-Muslim polity, as will be shown later. It is only as an incident in a much wider scheme, however, that it is discussed.

It is the object of this essay, therefore, to analyze the relations between the Muslim world and the Frankish kingdom and to make a tentative restatement of the situation in the light of the available evidence and of the political theory of Perso-Muslim monarchy.

The political setting arises primarily from two causes: the hostility of the house of Saint Arnulf to the Umayyads in Spain, and the rivalry of the house of 'Abbās with the Umayyads in the East, which resulted in an attempt to wrest the western province of Spain from the Umayyad cause. In addition, there was in the East the secular conflict between Rome and Persia, Persia's 'Rūmī feud,' continued in the 'Abbāsids' wars to enforce their claim to overlordship over the Eastern Empire,[1] and complicated by Papal antagonism to Constantinople and the iconoclastic policy of the Isaurian Emperors.[2] The former factors supply the Muslim motive for the relations, the latter provide the means through which the relations came into being. In order to collect the threads of the diplomacy, it is necessary to go back to the battle of the Zāb in 750, when the Umayyad Khalīfah Marwān was overthrown by 'Abdu'llāh, the general of

---

[1] Cf. Mas'ūdī, no. 33, p. 427; Ibnu'l-Ṭiqṭaqā, no. 23a, pp. 38–39, 306; no. 23b, pp. 48, 384; Müller, no. 119, I, 485.
[2] Cf. Hefele-LeClercq, no. 102, pp. 710–714, 725.

Abū'l-'Abbās, who proceeded to establish his house in the Succession of the Prophet, and to earn the self-assumed title of Al-Saffāḥ—the Bloody—by systematic slaughter of the remnants of the fallen house of Umayya and its supporters. Marwān was slain in Egypt, and of the descendants of Hishām one alone survived, 'Abdu'l-Raḥmān, who, after many adventures and narrow escapes, ultimately found his way to Spain.[1]

There he found the Muslim conquerors divided into two main camps, the Qaisites under Ṣumail and the Yamanites. The Qaisites had been among the first to revolt against the Umayyads, and Ṣumail had no desire to see a member of that house in power. On the other hand, the Yamanites welcomed a leader of their cause, and 'Abdu'l-Raḥmān was able to establish himself by means of their support.[2] In the years preceding his arrival, however, news of the 'Abbāsid revolution had reached Spain, and 'Amr, a Quraish of Cordova, had announced his appointment by the 'Abbāsid Khalīfah to the governorship of Spain (753–754) in opposition to the Yamanite party.[3] Meanwhile, in the year 752, probably in order to escape the concerted action of the Yamanite forces, Sulaimān, the *walī* of Barcelona and the Gironde, had acknowledged Pippin I as his protector and overlord.[4] Consequently, even before the arrival of 'Abdu'l-Raḥmān, the king of the Franks had become to some extent the avowed protector of the anti-Yamanite—that is, the 'Abbāsid—

[1] Ibnu'l-Ṭiqṭaqā, no. 23a, pp. 203–205; no. 23b, pp. 240–243; Dozy, no. 84, pp. 161 ff.; Huart, no. 103, I, 285–286, 288–289; Muir, no. 120, pp. 428–430; Browne, no. 65, I, pp. 244–247.

[2] The Qaisite hostility to the Banū Quraish antedates the advent of Islām (Huart, no. 103, I, 92), and the Banū Qais were among the early rebels against the Umayyads (Dozy, no. 84, pp. 65 ff.; *Cambridge Medieval History*, no. 78, II, 363); for the Yamanite antagonism to the 'Abbāsids, cf. Ibnu'l-Ṭiqṭaqā, no. 23a, pp. 235–236; no. 23b, pp. 287–288 and n. 1; for the situation in Spain in 751 and the following years, *Cambridge Medieval History*, no. 78, III, 409–412; Dozy, no. 84, pp. 137–160, 167 ff.; Nöldeke, no. 121, pp. 107 ff., 112; Huart, no. 103, II, 141–145; Lembke, no. 113, I, 327 ff.; Fauriel, no. 89, III, 244; Al-Makkārī, no. 29, II, 421, n. 22.

[3] Dozy, no. 84, pp. 158 ff., 177–178; Lembke, no. 113, I, p. 294, n. 1, gives the titles as *walī* (*praepositus*), *amīr* (*princeps*), and *'āmil* (*gubernator*). This is not strictly correct, for the *'āmil* appears to have been primarily a revenue officer under the *dīwān*, and probably the only titles applicable to the officers who came in contact with Charles were the first and second.

[4] *Annales Mettenses*, no. 8, a.752, p. 331; *Chronicon Moissiacense*, no. 13, a.751, p. 294; cf. Dorr, no. 82, p. 10, n. 34; Oelsner, no. 122, p. 340, n. 5; Lembke, no. 113, I, pp. 300 ff., 343 f.; Dahn, no. 81, III, 789, 863–864, 918; Dozy, no. 84, pp. 156–158; Fauriel, no. 89, III, 246–248, places this event erroneously in 759.

cause in Spain.¹ In this way, the relations of Pippin with Spain took their place in the domain of Muslim politics just at the time of the Berber rising in North Africa, which resulted in the capture of Qairuwān by the 'Abbāsids in 761,² and eleven years prior to that fatal expedition of 'Alā ibn Mughīth against Spain in 763, which compelled the Khalīfah Al-Manṣūr to cast about for assistance in the task of subduing the rebel province.³

To the north of the Pyrenees, a parallel state of affairs existed. Southern Gaul had never acquiesced in the rise of the Mayors of the Palace.⁴ Count Eudo of Aquitaine had given his daughter to a Berber chief, presumably to strengthen his position against Charles Martel (730),⁵ and Maurontus, count of Marseilles, handed over Arles, Avignon, and other towns to the Muslim *amīr* of Narbonne. The last expedition of Charles (739)⁶ was not against the Saracens but against Maurontus, who fled. The coronation of Pippin in 752 is the counterpart of the 'Abbāsid succession in Baghdād, and the supplanting of the Merovingian Childerich III by the son of Charles

¹ Fauriel, no. 89, III, p. 247, noticed the development of Spanish affairs, but he failed to connect it with the 'Abbāsid cause. His judgment is as follows: 'Il y a beaucoup d'apparence que le motif de Soliman était de se soustraire à l'autorité d'Abd el Rahman ben Mouayia et de se maintenir indépendant dans le commandement de l'Espagne orientale sous la protection nominale ou réelle du roi des Francs.'
² Huart, no. 103, I, 296.
³ Oelsner, no. 122, p. 396; Huart, no. 103, I, 296, II, 146–147; Dozy, no. 84, pp. 199 ff. In addition to the trouble in Spain, Al-Manṣūr was threatened at home by an 'Alid revolt in favour of the Umayyads. See Ibnu'l-Ṭiqṭaqā, no. 23a, pp. 222–226; no. 23b, pp. 268–275.
⁴ On the jealousy of the older nobility toward the upstart house of Saint Arnulf, see Dahn, no. 81, III, 919 ff.
⁵ Isidore Pacensis, no. 25, cols. 1245. ff., 'Et quia filiam suam dux Francorum nomine Eudo causa foederis ei in coniugio copulandam ob persecutionem Arabum differendam iam olim tradiderat ad suos libitus inclinandam, dum eam tardidat de manu persequentium liberandam, suam morti debitam praeparat animam.' Cf. *Annales Laur. Min.* no. 7, pp. 725–726, 730; *Gesta Abb. Font.* no. 20, p. 282; *Chron. Moiss*, no. 13, a. 752; Gibbon, no. 94, VI, 18, n. 38; Breysig, no. 62, pp. 61–66; Fauriel, no. 89, III, 102 ff., 147 ff.; on Eudo's share in promoting the Saracen invasion, Breysig, *Annales Fuldenses*, no. 6, a. 725 (following *Annales Mettenses*, no. 8, or *Annales Laur. Min.*, no. 7), attribute the invasion of 731 to Eudo's invitation: 'Sarraceni ab Eudone in auxilium suum vocati cum rege suo Abdirama Garonnam Burdigalemque pervenient cunctis locis vastatis et aeclesiis igne crematis. . . .' On the significance of the surrender of a daughter, see Buckler, no. 67, p. 243.
⁶ Cf. *Annales Fuldenses*, no. 6 (following *Annales Laur. Min.*, no. 7) a. 738: 'Carolus regionem Provinciam ingressus Maurontum ducem qui dudum Sarracenos per dolum invitaverat fugere compulit,' Continuator Fredegarii, no. 14, c. 109; Breysig, no. 62, pp. 7, n. 4, 84.

Martel served only to intensify the feud between the house of Charles and the Southern counts, so that 'Abdu'l-Raḥmān found in Waifar of Aquitaine an ally against his Frankish opponent.[1] The capture of Narbonne by the Franks in 759 completed the work of the battle of Tours (732) and brought the frontier of Pippin's kingdom into direct contact with the territory of the *walī* of Barcelona, which was, theoretically at least, under Frankish protection.[2] The years 760 to 768 were occupied mainly with the suppression of Waifar,[3] and with the development of the Franco-Papal alliance against Constantinople, which constitutes the third strand in the negotiations.

The policy of the Papacy at this time was to prevent any alliance between Pippin and Constantinople. Pippin had sent a mission to Constantine V Copronymus in 757, and the Emperor had responded with a return mission; but though mutual friendship was pledged, no definite results followed.[4] When another mission from Constantinople arrived at Pippin's court in 765, Pope Paul I wrote to Pippin, urging him not only to insist on the recognition of the primacy of the see of Rome and on reverence for images, but also to detain the ambassadors until he could call a council at Rome.[5] In another letter of the same period, Paul complains bitterly of the intrigue of the Greeks in Italy,[6] while a third encloses for Pippin's perusal a letter from Cosmas, Patriarch of Alexandria.[7] This letter is undated, and Hefele states, without quoting any authority, that it was received in Rome in the August following the death of Paul. This must be a mistake. The letter cannot very well be a copy of the *Libellus*

[1] Dahn, no. 81, III, 789; Breysig, no. 62, pp. 142–144; Oelsner, no. 122, p. 396; Fauriel, no. 89, III, 233 ff.

[2] Continuator Fredegarii, no. 14, c. 127; *Chronicon Moissiacense*, no. 13, 1. 759; Dahn, no. 81, III, 919.

[3] *Annales Regni Francorum*, no. 11, a. 760–768; Continuator Fredegarii, no. 14, c. 134; for the campaigns, Oelsner, no. 122, pp. 338–413; Dahn, no. 81, III, 925–944.

[4] Hefele-LeClercq, no. 102, pp. 713–714; Cont. Fred., no. 14, c. 123. 'Nescio quo faciente, postea amicitia, quam inter se mutuo promiserant, nullatenus sortita est effectum.' The objects of the mission and the attitude of Pope Stephen III are set out in his letter to Pippin (Jaffé, no. 26, pp. 65–66; *Epp. Mer. et Kar.*, no. 16, pp. 506–507; cf. Oelsner, no. 122, pp. 346–347).

[5] Jaffé, no. 26, pp. 109–110, 130–132; *Epp. Mer. et Kar.*, no. 16, pp. 534–535, 548–549.

[6] Jaffé, no. 26, p. 137; *Epp. Mer. et Kar.*, no. 16, p. 551. Cf. Hefele-LeClercq, no. 102, pp. 711 ff., for Byzantine efforts to hold Italy and the West.

[7] See Appendix II.

Synodicus of John the Goth nor the letter so frequently quoted by Hadrian, but it must have been of interest to Pippin.[1] It must be read, too, in relation with the policy of Constantine Copronymus. I suggest that it is the proceedings of the Council of the Three Patriarchs against Cosmas, bishop of Epiphania, who had gone over to the Iconoclasts. The date of the Council is Whitsunday, 763, and the letter would presumably reach Rome, and probably reach Pippin, before 765.[2] Further, it is stated by Eutychius of Alexandria that Cosmas owed his elevation to the patriarchate of Alexandria, over the heads of his heretical rivals, to the direct intervention of the Khalīfah Hishām. This fact would presuppose his friendly relations with the Muḥammadan authorities and a close attachment to the Khalīfah's court.[3] In these circumstances, it would seem not impossible that the letter also contained the suggestion of a mission to Baghdād. At the synod of Attigny it was decided to dispatch such a mission, for another event had indicated to Pippin the desirability of the step.

In 763, 'Alā ibn Mughīth, sent by Al-Manṣūr to bring Spain to the 'Abbāsid allegiance, landed at Beja and united with the opponents of 'Abdu'l-Raḥmān. The attempt, however, proved a disastrous failure. 'Alā ibn Mughīth and his associates were defeated before Toledo and executed. Al-Manṣūr's *farmān*, the 'Abbāsid standard, and the heads of the insurgents were returned to the Khalīfah at Baghdād. Al-Manṣūr is reported to have thanked God for placing the sea between him and such a foe.[4]

[1] Hefele-LeClercq, no. 102, pp. 723 ff.

[2] Hefele-LeClercq, no. 102, pp. 723–725. If the letter was written as a result of the Council, it cannot have been sent to Pippin 'before 762,' as Langen states (no. 112, I, 659). As the date of the Council was Whitsunday, 763, there seems to be no reason why it should not have reached Pope Paul I early in 764 at the latest; the evidence for the time taken in the journey can be deduced from the movements of the monk Zacharias in 799–800.

[3] Eutychius, no. 18, II, 385–387. Theodore of Antioch had been exiled in 757 on the suspicion of correspondence with Constantinople (Theophanes, no. 45, I, 430). He was the son of the deputy of Arabia Minor (*ibid.*, p. 427). He succeeded Theophylact as Patriarch in the ninth year of Constantine V (749) and, if Eutychius is correct, ruled until 769. For the bitterness of Christians against Constantine, see Michael Syrus, no. 36, II, 517–522; III, 2, 12 (bk. xi, cc. 24 ff.; xii). For Muslim influence in Christian affairs, see *ibid.*, II, 511 (bk. xi, c. 22). Nöldeke points out that 'it was certainly easier for a man to live as a Christian under the rule of the Caliphs than as a Christian heretic within the Byzantine Empire.' No. 121, p. 86.

[4] Dozy, no. 84, pp. 198–199. Note the relations between Hishām ibn 'Udhra and the Ya-

The incident is important for two reasons. First, it is not improbable that the news of the attempt of the 'Abbāsids to overthrow 'Abdu'l-Raḥmān reached Pippin, and, secondly, its failure and sequel would predispose Al-Manṣūr in favour of the Frankish mission when it reached Baghdād. Whatever the source of the suggestion may have been, the antagonism between Rome and Constantinople and the Frankish support of Papal policy must have been the determining factors in the decision to seek the friendship of the Byzantine Emperor's principal enemy. Consequently, in 765, Pippin dispatched a mission to Baghdād. Three years later it returned, accompanied by ambassadors of the Khalīfah and bearing many presents.[1] The nature of the presents will be discussed later; it is sufficient here to notice that the Saracens were well received by Pippin, who dismissed them with presents, and that they returned to their country by sea. The year 768 was also marked by the death of

---

manites. *Ibid.*, p. 199, also Nöldeke, *loc. cit.* 'Alā ibn Mughīth appears to have been sent to Spain by Muḥammad ibnu'l-Ash'ath, with the 'Abbāsid fleet, shortly after the capture of Cairo (August 1, 761), and not by Al-Manṣūr, who, however, sent to Mughīth the black banner of the 'Abbāsids, an act which may be regarded as a confirmation of the action of Ibnu'l-Ash'ath. Barthold, no. 56, p. 268, following Ibn 'Adhārī, no. 21, II, 53 ff., 60, 62, and the anonymous Akhbār Majmū'at, no. 3, p. 102. Barthold's implied attack (*loc. cit.*, p. 268) on Vasiliev's position, that Al-Manṣūr's reign was not the heyday of the Caliphate, and therefore not the time for any attack on so distant a region as Spain, appears to break down before the fact of Al-Manṣūr's general policy to restore order. See Nöldeke, no. 121, pp. 124–129, 139–143. Barthold (*Khristianski Vostok*, I, 82 ff., III, 284 f., quoting Ṭabarī, III, 646, continues this argument to cover the Barmakid period, when Hārūn was forced to leave Ḥīra for Kūfa in 796, on account of attacks on him, and argues, further, 'that the assumption that the Caliph could communicate with remote parts of the empire by letter or envoy presupposes a state of affairs which did not exist.' On this basis he develops his contention that the only possible official source (if any) for the embassies was derived from the local officials in Palestine or from the Aghlabids in Egypt.

[1] Cont. Fred., no. 14, c. 134. 'Nunciatum est regi quod myssos suos quos dudum ad Amormuni regi Saracinorum misserat, post tres annos ad Marsiliam reversus fuisset.' *Amormuni = Amīru'l-Mūminīn*, the Leader of the Faithful, the principal title and office of the *Khalīfatu' rasūli-llāhi*, the successor of the Prophet of God. Oelsner observes, 'Das Verbot des Koran, in einen Bund mit Ungläubigen zu treten, hinderte Manssur nicht, sich zunächst in diplomatische Beziehungen mit Pippin einzulassen.' No. 122, p. 396; cf. also Joranson, no. 107, p. 258, n. 75. But it must be observed that the implication of a vassal status would remove the objection. E. A. Freeman, no. 92, p. 257, assigns the initiative to Al-Manṣūr. For further discussion see Dahn, no. 81, III, 939–940; Müller, no. 119, I, 464 f.; Fauriel, no. 89, III, 330; Abel and Simson, no. 51, p. 228, and n. 1; *infra*, pp. 32 ff. This assumption meets Barthold's objection (no. 56, p. 269, and n. 2).

Pippin and the accession of Charles and Carloman. It may be useful, therefore, to sum up the diplomatic situation at the death of Pippin.

The Pope, secure in the support of the patriarchates of Jerusalem, Antioch, and Alexandria, was committed to a feud with Constantinople on the question of image worship.[1] He was secure, too, in the support of Pippin, who had resisted the 'blandishments' and 'abundance of promises' of Constantine Copronymus.[2] In the East, the home of the Caliphate (*dāru'l-Khilāfat*) had been removed from Damascus to Baghdād, with the result that the 'Abbāsids came to inherit the feud of the Persian kings of the house of Sāsān against the Roman Empire. In the wars that followed, beginning with 'Abdu'-llāh's invasion of 754, this hostility gradually developed on the side of the 'Abbāsids into a claim to overlordship, and Ibnu'l-Ṭiqṭaqā refers to the continuous disobedience of the Byzantine Emperors during the reigns of Al-Manṣūr and his successors.[3] Since Pippin, king of the Franks, was not only the champion of the Papacy against the Isaurian Emperors at Constantinople, but also the guardian of the 'Abbāsid interests in Spain against the Umayyads,[4] the diplomatic mission of 765 to Baghdād served to complete a circle of alliances ranging the Pope, the 'Abbāsid Khalīfah, and the king of the Franks against the Umayyads and Constantinople.[5] The constitutional effect of the mission from Al-Manṣūr, as will appear later, was to render legitimate Pippin's overlordship over Saragossa and Barcelona by including him among his *Umarā*. In other words, Pippin's position, according to 'Abbāsid constitutional theory and practice, was that of the Khalīfah's *amīr* over Spain in succession to 'Alā ibn Mughīth.[6]

Then came a break in the continuity of Carolingian diplomacy. For

---

[1] Dahn, no. 81, III, 929-930; Hefele-LeClercq, no. 102, pp. 724-725, 952; Jaffé, no. 26, pp. 126, 138-139, 153-154; *Epp. Mer. et Kar.*, no. 16, pp. 545, 552-553, 652-653.

[2] Jaffé, no. 26, pp. 126, 149 ff.; *Epp. Mer. et Kar.*, no. 16, pp. 545, 650 ff.; *Ann. Laur. Min.*, no. 7, a. 767; Oelsner, no. 122, p. 404.

[3] For a summary of events, see Müller, no. 119, I, 485; Huart, no. 103, I, 279 ff.; Ibnu'l-Ṭiqṭaqā, no. 23a, pp. 38-39; no. 23b, pp. 47-48.

[4] Oelsner, no. 122, p. 397; Dahn, no. 81, III, 789, 939.

[5] Cf. Finlay, no. 90, II, 50 f.

[6] See *infra*, pp. 32 ff.

nine years Muslim affairs fell into the background. For Pope Stephen IV the opening years of the reign of Charles the Great were fraught with considerable anxiety, for it was not clear whether Charles intended to pursue a Germanic policy, involving an alliance with the Lombard king, Desiderius, whose daughter he married in 770, or whether he would continue his father's policy of supporting the Papacy.[1] The divorce of the Lombard wife in 771, however, marks his decision to adhere to the latter policy, while the death of his brother Carloman in the same year left him supreme in the Frankish realm. With the accession of Hadrian I to the Papal throne in 772 begins an alliance between Charles and the Papacy which lasted to the king's death. The next five years of the reign of Charles were occupied with Saxon and Lombard wars, ending in the pacification of Saxony by the synod of Paderborn in 777.[2] In the meantime, the position of 'Abdu'l-Raḥmān ibn Mu'āwiya was threatened by the connection of the 'Abbāsid party with the revolt of the Berbers in Central Spain. The revolt was organized by three confederates: the *walī* of Barcelona, Sulaimān ibn Yaqdhānu'l-A'rābī, whose *wilāyat* was already under Frankish protection; 'Abdu'l-Raḥmān ibn Ḥabīb, whose family was identified with the opposition to the Umayyad cause; and Abū'l-Aswad ibn Yūsuf, whose father had been imprisoned by 'Abdu'l-Raḥmān ibn Mu'āwiya. Their plan involved the raising of auxiliary levies from the African Berbers, and had it succeeded, 'Abdu'l-Raḥmān would have been cut off completely from the Mediterranean. To strengthen the northern contingent of the rebels, Sulaimān and his son Yūsuf went in person to Charles at Paderborn in 777 and placed themselves and their territories under his protection.[3] The plan miscarried, owing to lack of coördination

[1] Cf. Stephen IV's letter, Jaffé, no. 26, pp. 158 ff.; *Epp. Mer. et Kar.*, no. 16, pp. 560 ff.; Einhard, no. 15, c. 18; Hefele-LeClercq, no. 102, pp. 953–955.

[2] For the attempt of Hadrian to arouse the antagonism of Charles against the Eastern Empire, see Jaffé, no. 26, p. 192; *Epp. Mer. et Kar.*, no. 16, pp. 582–583.

[3] For the details of the conspiracy, see Lembke, no. 113, I, 314 f.; 345 f.; Dozy, no. 84, pp. 165 ff., 204 ff.; Huart, no. 103, II, 145–146; Fauriel, no. 89, III, 322 ff.; Abel and Simson, no. 51, pp. 216, 228–233; Dahn, no. 81, III, 984 ff. *Annales Einhardi*, no. 11, a. 777: 'Venit eodem in loco ac tempore ad regis praesentiam de Hispania Sarraceni quidam nomine Ibin al arabi cum aliis Sarracenis sociis suis, dedens se ac civitates quibus eum rex Sarracenus praefecerat.' *Ann. Laur. Min.*, no. 7, a. 777: 'Etiam ad eundem placitum venerunt Sarraceni de partibus Hispaniae, hii sunt Ibnalarabi et filius Deiuzefi qui et latine Joseph nominatur, similiter et genus eius.'

and to the mutual mistrust of the conspirators, which made it possible for 'Abdu'l-Raḥmān to deal with each of his opponents separately. Before Charles could arrive in Spain, Ibn Ḥabīb had landed at Tadmīr and raised the standard of the 'Abbāsid Khalīfah; but instead of uniting his strength with that of the *walī* of Barcelona, Ibn Ḥabīb, believing that he had turned traitor to the cause, proceeded to attack him. He may, of course, have regarded the action of Sulaimān in approaching the infidel Charles as an act of treason to Islām. Whatever reason he had for his action, the step proved fatal to his cause. Sulaimān defeated the attack; and 'Abdu'l-Raḥmān, after procuring the assassination of Ibn Ḥabīb in the same year, was left free to deal with Sulaimān and his Frankish ally. Sulaimān was thus obliged to face alone the whole of the Umayyad army; for Abū'-l-Aswad's support proved to be too feeble for notice by any chronicler, either Arabic or Latin.[1] His sole hope of success, therefore, lay in the support of Charles, but owing to his misjudgment of Muslim opinion, this support proved a handicap rather than a help. The invasion of Muslim territory by the unbeliever Charles laid upon every believer the obligation to wage war (*jihād*) against him, so that when Sulaimān, after taking Saragossa, attempted to admit Charles to the city, Muslim opinion was outraged. Charles, disillusioned by his reception, decided to return to his own kingdom, taking with him Ibnu'l-A'rābī in chains, (et ipsum Ebilarbium vinctum duxit in Franciam). It seems clear that this was the cause of his abandonment of the expedition, and not the rebellion of Widukind, of which he did not hear, if Einhard is to be trusted, until he reached Autun. On his return occurred the famous attack of the Basques on his rearguard at Roncesvalles (778).[2] So ended Charles's first expedition to Spain. There was no crusading motive present,

---

Ann. Fuld., no. 6, a. 777: 'Et conventus in Saxonia habitus in loco qui vocatur Padrabrunno; ubi Ibinalarabi Sarracenus praefectus Caesaraugustae venit ad regem.' Sulaimān was *walī* of Barcelona, not Saragossa: Lembke, no. 113, I, 345, n. 1.

[1] Dozy, no. 84, p. 205. Barthold (no. 56, p. 269) contends that the Frankish king could not find as many followers as Al-Mughīth in 763. He overlooks, however, the fact that the insurgents were relying on his Frankish army.

[2] For the collapse and consequences of the revolt, see Dozy, no. 84, pp. 205–206. The *Annales Einhardi*, no. 11, a. 778, clearly separate the rebellion of Widukind ('interea Saxones, velut occasionem nancti, sumptis armis ad Rhenum usque profecti sunt') from the causes of

nor was any attributed to it prior to 840. In the *Annales Einhardi* the motive was 'the hope of taking certain cities in Spain.' The 'persuasion' came from the Saracen, the blessing from the Pope.[1] It was not until the stormy days following the death of Louis the Pious that the biographer of Louis stated that the expedition was intended to help 'the church labouring under the bitter yoke of the Saracens,'[2] and not until the end of the tenth century was Einhard's 'ex persuasione praedicti Sarraceni' transformed by the Chronicler of Metz into 'motus precibus et querelis Christianorum.'[3] To Charles the failure of this expedition may have suggested the desirability of entering into diplomatic relations with the 'Abbāsids as his father had done in order to obtain a proper standing in the eyes of the Muslimīn. This course of action would at least merit the consideration of Charles if the abandonment of the expedition was due to the repugnance of the Muslimīn to his entry into Saragossa, while it would be to Ibnu'l-A'rābī's interest to suggest it.[4]

'Abdu'l-Rahmān then marched against Saragossa, which capitulated; Sulaimān was assassinated as a traitor to the Muslim cause; Abū'l-Aswad was defeated at the battle of the Guadilamar; and the

---

Charles's retirement ('cuius rei nuncium est cum rex apud Autesiodorum civitatem accepisset'); so too *Annales Petaviani*, no. 10, p. 16, and *Ann. Laur. Min.*, no. 7, a. 778. Einhard's statement is that Charles reached Saragossa, for which he accepted hostages (i.e., he did not enter or take possession of the city), and retired to Pampeluna, 'cuius muros, ne debellare posset, ad solum usque destruxit, ac regredi statuens, Pyrinei saltum ingressus est.' Cf. Reinaud, no. 128, p. 95, n. 1.

[1] No. 11, a. 778: 'Tunc ex persuasione praedicti Sarraceni spem capiendarum quarundem in Hispania civitatum haud frustra concipiens, congregato exercitu profectus est.' Hadrian wrote, 'Inter ea petimus te, magnae rex et dulcissime fili ... ut angelus Dei omnipotentis vos praecedat, et faciat vestra praecellentia triumfans atque cum magnis victoriis et exaltationem ad proprii regni vestri culmen una cum omnem Deo dilectum Francorum exercitum incolumem revertendam.' Jaffé, no. 26, p. 201; *Epp. Mer. et Kar.*, no. 16, p. 588.

[2] *Vita Hludovici Pii*, no. 47, p. 608: 'Laboranti ecclesiae sub Sarracenorum acerbissimo iugo.' The date of the *Vita* is, at the earliest, 838–840. See Wattenbach, no. 133, I, 203; Manitius, no. 117, I, 655–657.

[3] *Ann. Mett.*, no. 8, a. 778, p. 158; these annals belong to the end of the tenth century (Wattenbach, no. 133, pp. 209–210).

[4] The account in the *Annales Einhardi* is significantly silent on the ill success of the alliance; but the exaction of hostages followed by the destruction of the walls of Pampeluna suggests the displeasure of Charles (cf. *supra*, p. 12). In the light of the history of Muslim intrigue with Frankish vassals, the possibility of Muslim instigation of the attack of the Basques at Roncesvalles may be suggested.

Basques and the Christian count of Cerdaña were made tributary to the Umayyads of Cordova. So, after a quarter of a century's struggle, 'Abdu'l-Raḥmān completed his conquest of Spain, except Asturias and Galicia, earning the admiration even of the Khalīfah Al-Manṣūr.[1] He had already, on the advice of 'Abdu'l-Mālik ibn 'Umar, a descendant of the Umayyad Khalīfah Marwān, declared his independence by the omission of the 'Abbāsid Khalīfah's name from the *Khuṭba* (c. 757), and although he contented himself with the title *Amīr*, and he and his successors until 929, when 'Abdu'l-Raḥmān III assumed the title of *Amīru'l-Mūminīn*, did not assume the title and rôle of Khalīfah, yet Spain was really from 757 onwards the headquarters of the Umayyad Caliphate, and the *Amīrs* of Cordova perpetuated the claim by the use of the title 'sons of the Khalīfah.'[2] 'Abdu'l-Raḥmān died in 788, and was succeeded by his son Hishām (788–796).[3]

In the East, the Emperor Constantine V had been compelled in 771 or 772 to make peace with the Khalīfah Al-Manṣūr at the price of payment of tribute, which was apparently regarded as a mark of vassaldom by the 'Abbāsids.[4] The peace, however, was short-lived, for in 775 'Abbāsid troops under Thumāma advanced along the Isaurian coast and besieged Syce. The deaths of the Emperor Constantine and the Khalīfah Al-Manṣūr in the same year were followed by greater activity on both sides.[5] The Khalīfah Al-Mahdī crossed the Euphrates at the head of 100,000 men and reached Aleppo, whence he despatched his son Hārūn along the coast to the Bosphorus. The campaign was so successful that, besides the heavy spoil, the Khalīfah was able to add to his treasures the tribute of

---

[1] Dozy, no. 84, pp. 205–206; Huart, no. 103, II, 146; Al-Makkārī, no. 29, II, 83–85.

[2] 'Abdu'l-Raḥmān III appears to have been the first to assume the title of Khalīfatu' Rasūli'llāhi. *Camb. Med. Hist.*, no. 78, III, 421, 430; Dozy, no. 84, p. 423; Huart, no. 103, II, 145, 154. Although Barthold, Vasiliev, and Joranson refer to Spanish affairs, none of them appears to have given them adequate recognition.

[3] For estimates of 'Abdu'l-Raḥmān, see Mas'ūdī, no. 33, pp. 427–428; Huart, no. 103, II, 147; Dozy, no. 84, pp. 207–211; *Camb. Med. Hist.*, no. 78, III, 413–414; *Enc. Islām*, no. 87, *sub nomine*. For an excellent summary of the politics of this period, see Zaydan, no. 135, pp. 268–270.

[4] Brooks, no. 64, XV, 734; see *supra*, p. 10.

[5] *Camb. Med. Hist.*, no. 78, III, 123.

Constantinople—the only terms on which the ambassadors of the Empress-Regent Irene could obtain peace in 781.[1]

The position of Irene was rendered more precarious by lack of support at home and by the antagonism of the West. To remedy this weakness, she attempted to form an alliance with Charles, to be cemented by the marriage of Rotrud to Constantine VI.[2] In order to remove the Pope's objections to the match, she proceeded to restore image worship, and to procure the election of Tarasius to the Patriarchate of Constantinople, with directions to summon a General Council there to discuss the whole question of images.[3]

The position of Hadrian I at this turn of events is interesting. While he apparently encouraged Irene in her efforts to restore image worship,[4] he was as apprehensive as any of his predecessors of the effects of an alliance between the courts of Byzantium and Aachen. He therefore kept Charles informed of the relations between Irene and the 'Abbāsids and of the affairs of Persia.[5] He also wrote at length on the subject of Greek intrigue in Italy, particularly among the disaffected Lombard vassals of the South.[6] In 785, there arrived in Rome an embassy announcing the elevation of Tarasius to the Patriarchate of Constantinople; in the following year, the bishops of the Byzantine Empire were summoned to attend the seventh oecumenical Council at Nicaea to decide the question of image worship.[7] In 787, Irene sent a mission to Charles to claim the hand of Rotrud, but at Capua it was stopped by the news that Constantine had already married Theodote, one of his mother's maids of honour.

[1] Brooks, no. 64, xv, 737–739; Bury, no. 73, ii, 484, 492. The sources for the treaty are Theophanes, no. 45, p. 456; Leo Grammaticus, no. 28, p. 193; Cedrenus, no. 12, ii, 21; Zonaras, no. 50, bk. xv, c. 10; Abū'l-Faraj, no. 2, 165 A.H.; idem, no. 1, a. 783.

[2] Theophanes, no. 45, p. 455; Leo Grammaticus, no. 28, p. 193; *Ann. Mosell.*, no. 9, a. 781, p. 497.

[3] Hefele-LeClercq, no. 102, pp. 446–447; Bury, no. 73, ii, 495–496; Abel and Simson, no. 51, i, 384; Harnack, no. 98, pp. 14 ff.

[4] Jaffé-Wattenbach, no. 105, i, nos. 2448, 2449.

[5] Jaffé, no. 26, p. 230; *Epp. Mer. et Kar.*, no. 16, p. 605.

[6] Hadrian had already written to Charles on this subject in 779–780. Jaffé, no. 26, pp. 210 ff.; *Epp. Mer. et Kar.*, no. 16, pp. 592–593. His later letters on the topic appear immediately after the arrival of the Byzantine mission of 785. Jaffé, no. 26, pp. 250, 252 ff.; *Epp. Mer. et Kar.*, no. 16, pp. 609 ff., 612 ff.

[7] Jaffé-Wattenbach, no. 105, i, no. 2448; Theophanes, no. 45, p. 460; Hefele-LeClercq, no. 102, pp. 448 ff., 700 ff.

Apparently the match was made with the connivance of Irene, who wished to discredit Constantine in the eyes of the clergy. So the betrothal with Rotrud was broken off.[1] In the latter part of this year an imperial mission was sent to Arichis of Beneventum, to invest him with the robes of the patriciate as a vassal of Constantine VI. Hadrian promptly informed Charles of the whole conspiracy, which he had extracted from the presbyter Gregorius, whose words he quoted.[2] Arichis, however, had died before the mission arrived, and Grimoald succeeded him, August 27, 787.[3] Grimoald refused to give a daughter in marriage to Constantine VI, who consequently ordered Theodore, the governor of Sicily, to devastate Beneventum. Grimoald, therefore, turned for help to Charles, who attacked Theodore, defeated the Greeks, and annexed Istria.[4] But Charles was called to the North again, and for the next seven years was kept busy by the Avars and the Saxons, so that he was obliged to neglect the affairs of the East.

[1] On the dispatch and arrival of the mission see *Ann. Einhardi*, no. 11, a. 786; on the breakdown of the negotiations, *Ann. Fuld.*, no. 6, a. 787 (from *Annales Sithienses*), 'Hruodthrudis filia regis a Constantino imperatore desponsatur;' L. M. Hartmann, no. 100, pt. 2, p. 304

[2] Jaffé, no. 26, pp. 269 ff.; *Epp. Mer. et Kar.*, no. 16, p. 617; Abel and Simson, no. 51, I, 605, 615; Bury, no. 74, pp. 311 f.; Dahn, no. 81, III, 1002 ff.

[3] Hartmann, no. 100, pt. 2, p. 307.

[4] *Ibid.*, pp. 307–308.

II

FRANCO-'ABBASID RELATIONS UNDER HARUNU'L-RASHID

IN 785, the Khalīfah Al-Mahdī died. After the short reign of his brother Al-Hādī, Hārūnu'l-Rashīd succeeded in 787. During his reign, the influence of Persia on the ceremonial of the 'Abbāsids became so marked that Maqrīzī assigns to this reign the first case of the gift of a robe of honour (*khil'at*) as a mark of official investiture in the Muslim state. In this detail he is probably in error; but the statement is significant, as it shows how closely connected were the sons of Al-Mahdī with the 'Medizing' of the Caliphate.¹ Hārūn had already won fame as a successful general against the Greeks, and he continued to wage war upon them after his accession. In 790, his admirals successfully attacked Crete and Cyprus, and the following years were signalized by frontier raids upon the Byzantine Empire, culminating in the invasion of the year 796. Hārūn then led an army as far as Ephesus and Ancyra, and concluded a four years' peace with the Empress Irene, on condition that she paid tribute (798). In the same year Irene sent a mission to Charles, surrendering all claims to Beneventum and Istria, but retaining her claim to Croatia. It is clear that she felt the need of support both against local factions and against Hārūnu'l-Rashīd.² It was probably in connection with these events that Theoctistus, the ambassador of Nicetas, governor of Sicily, visited Charles in 797 at Aachen with a letter from Con-

[1] Dozy, no. 83, p. 14, n. 4, quotes the following passage from Maqrīzī:

واول من علمته خلع من اهل الدول جعفر بن يحيى البرمكي

('and among the men of the state, the first on whom a *khil'at* was conferred, I am told, was Ja'far, the son of Yaḥya, the Barmakid'). On the significance of this passage, see *infra*, pp. 33 ff. For a full discussion of the influence of Persian ideas and institutions on the development of the 'Abbāsid state, see Browne, no. 65, I, pp. 247, 255–260; Palmer, no. 123, pp. 18–19, 37, *et passim*.

[2] Huart, no. 103, I, 292 f., 295 ff.; for the mission to 'Abdu'l-Malik, Theophanes, no. 45, p. 473; and the peace with Hārūnu'l-Rashīd, Weil, no. 134, II, 157; Bury, no. 73, II, 493; the mission to Charles, surrendering all claim to Istria and Beneventum, but retaining Croatia, *Ann. Einhardi*, no. 11, a. 798–799; cf. Poeta Saxo, no. 40, p. 571 (bk. iii, vv. 403–426); Bury, no. 74, p. 317.

stantinople. Charles received him with full honours and allowed him to depart.[1] Among those present at Aachen was 'Abdu'llāh, son of 'Abdu'l-Raḥmān ibn Mu'āwiya. He had been exiled to Mauretania by his brother Hishām, who had succeeded their father in 788.[2] During the reign of Hishām (788–796) another issue arose to widen the breach between Spain and Baghdād. The jurist Mālik ibn Anas, the founder of the Mālikite school of jurisprudence, had been bastinadoed at Baghdād on account of the support he had given to an 'Alid pretender. He therefore left the 'Abbāsid court and made his way back to Medina. While he was there, 'several eminent doctors left Cordova and other cities in Andalus to make their pilgrimage to Mecca.' They made his acquaintance, and the support he gave to the pretensions of the Umayyads in Spain paved the way for the triumph of his school in the West.[3] In Hishām he professed to see the ideal Muslim prince, and declared that he alone was worthy of the throne of the Khilāfat.[4] In 796 Hishām died and was succeeded by his son, Al-Ḥakam (796–822), whose indifference to the Mālikites led in 805 to a plot to overthrow him and to set up in his place Ibn Shammās.[5] It was during these two reigns that the anti-Umayyad forces began to assert themselves. In 793, Hishām, hearing that Charles was absent owing to a Saxon rebellion, sent an army which captured Gerona and advanced as far as the river Orbieu. Checked there by the Margrave William, it returned home with much booty.[6] This fact, combined with the outbreak of the Felician

---

[1] *Ann. Laur. Min.*, no. 7, a. 797, p. 182.

[2] *Ann Einhardi*, no. 11, a. 797: 'Inde regressus cum Aquasgrani venisset, ibique Abdellam Sarracenum, filium Ibin-Mauge regis, de Mauritania ad se venientem suscepisset.' *Ann. Laur. Min*: 'et in Aquis palacio Abdellam Sarracenum filium Ibin-Mauge regis, qui a fratre regno pulsus in Mauretania exulabat, ipso seipsum commendante suscepit.'

[3] Al-Makkārī, no. 29, II, 100; on Al-Manṣūr's treatment of Mālik, see Dozy, no. 84, p. 243; Browne, no. 65, p. 295; Muir, no. 120, pp. 455–456; on his conservative position and his influence see MacDonald, no. 115, pp. 99–103; Fagnan, no. 88, pp. 107–109; Goldziher, no. 95, pp. 42, 52, 283; *Enc. Islām*, no. 87, *sub nomine*; *Kitāb el-Istiqça*, no. 27, I, 266 ff. Mālik ibn Anas died in 795.

[4] Dozy, no. 84, pp. 243–244.

[5] Dozy, no. 84, pp. 244 ff. This plot may account for the outbreak of hostilities in 806, which culminated in Al-Ḥakam's mission to Charles for peace in 810. See *infra*, p. 39.

[6] *Ann. Einhardi*, no. 11, a. 793; *Chron. Moiss.*, no. 13, a. 793, p. 300; *Vita Hlud. Pii*, no. 47, c. 5; Lembke, no. 113, I, 349 ff., 356 ff.

or Adoptionist heresy,[1] apparently brought Charles to the decision that firm measures against Cordova were necessary. He had already in 791 established the kingdom of Aquitaine under his infant son Louis.[2] In 794 at the Council of Frankfort, the Adoptionist heresy was condemned. The same council rejected the claim of the Council of Constantinople (787), which had condemned image worship, to be oecumenical.[3] After ecclesiastical affairs had been settled, Charles decided to continue his campaign on the Rhine while he sent Louis back to Aquitaine. In the following year he established the Spanish Mark, fortifying Ausona, Cardona, and Castaserra, and in 796 he dispatched a force which harried the North of Spain.[4] In 797, the *walī* of Barcelona, probably Zaid by name, having recently captured the city, handed it over to Charles. Charles then sent Louis to besiege Huesca, while he himself went against the Saxons.[5] It was on his return to Aachen that he received the exile 'Abdu'llāh, son of 'Abdu'l-Raḥmān ibn Mu'āwiya, who was still excluded from the succession and appears to have hoped to gain Frankish support against his nephew.[6] Another mission was also present at Aachen; King Alfonso of Asturias and Galicia, after a successful campaign, sent gifts and commended himself to Charles.[7]

In addition to these, Theoctistus, the ambassador of Nicetas, governor of Sicily, was also present, as has already been noticed, and Charles recalled Pippin from Italy and Louis from Aquitaine and Spain.[8] It would seem that it was at this time that Charles decided to send a mission to Baghdād, as his father had done thirty years

---

[1] The possibility of the Adoptionist heresy attracting the attention of Charles to Muslim affairs is suggested by Alcuin (no. 4, col. 234, quoted by Hefele-LeClercq, no. 102, p. 1003, q.v.), and it is his opinion, whether it is right or wrong, that is here the chief concern. It is necessary to point out that the rejection of Muslim influence by Harnack (no. 99, v, 281 and n. 4), and more emphatically by Hefele-LeClercq (no. 102, p. 1011) on the ground of Spanish Christian antipathy to Islām is a difficult position to maintain in the face of the evidence produced by Sir Thomas Arnold (no. 52, pp. 135 ff.).

[2] *Vita Hlud. Pii*, no. 47, c. 6.
[3] Hefele-LeClercq, no. 102, pp. 1045–60.
[4] *Ann. Reg. Franc.*, no. 11, a. 794; *Vita Hlud. Pii*, no. 47, c. 6.
[5] *Ann. Einhardi*, no. 11, a. 797; *Vita Hlud. Pii*, no. 47, c. 10; cf. Lembke, no. 113, I, p. 364, n. 2; Dahn, no. 81, III, 1058–59.
[6] See *supra*, p. 18.
[7] *Ann. Einhardi*, no. 11, a. 797.
[8] See *supra*, p. 17.

before.[1] There are several possible sources from which the suggestion may have come. First of all, the surrender of Barcelona may well have reminded Charles of his difficulties twenty years earlier, when the fate of Sulaimān and his own inability to gain admission into Saragossa had taught him the need of some form of authorization from the Khalīfah for his intervention in Muslim affairs. Zaid himself may have suggested the course.[2] Secondly, 'Abdu'llāh must have been acquainted with the course of events in the Muslim world and the prolonged efforts of the 'Abbāsids to establish their dominion over the West, which culminated in the appointment, two years later, of Ibrahīm ibnu'l-Aghlab as governor of Egypt.[3] Thirdly, there were the affairs of Constantinople. The contents of the letter from Constantinople are unknown, but it may have included a request to Charles to intervene with Hārūn for peace, while the death of Hadrian I in 795 had removed the most uncompromising opponent to a reconciliation between Charles and the East, and even Hadrian had not appeared entirely irreconcilable. Pope Leo III never appears to have commanded the respect or friendship of Charles as his predecessor had done. On the other hand, the idea of an alliance between Hārūn and Charles against the Empire may have been suggested by the course of events. The intrigues of the Greeks in Italy would have given adequate reason for reprisals. On the whole, however, these reasons are outweighed by the genuine efforts of Irene to overcome the hostility of the Franks, and by the unexpected peace with Irene in 798, followed by her offer of marriage with Charles to cement the two Empires or to give Charles the status

[1] The authorities give no indication that Charles was reminded of these events, but the inference seems permissible, *pace* Barthold (no. 56, p. 269) who objects to Vasiliev's suggestion (no. 132, pp. 77–80).

[2] Einhard's account contains the clue to the situation. After Barcelona had reverted to Saracen rule, 'tandem per Zatum Sarracenum, qui tunc eam invaserat, regi reddita est' (a. 797). The suggestion that he wished to avoid the fate of Sulaimān of Saragossa seems not improbable.

[3] 'Inde iterum ... Hludowicum ad Aquitaniam remisit, cum quo et Abdellam Sarracenum ire iussit, qui postea, ut ipse voluit, in Hispaniam ductus, et illorum fidei, quibus se credere non dubitavit, commissus est.' *Ann. Einhardi*, no. 11, a. 797. For further discussion of this passage see *infra*, p. 21, n. 1. On the state of affairs in Mauretania and Egypt see *Cam. Med. Hist.*, no. 78, IV, 275–276; Huart, no. 103, I, 296 f., 321 f.; II, 198.

of Emperor.[1] Finally, the connection of the mission with 'Abdu' llāh's visit appears to be established, in part by the reason already suggested, and partly by the fact that he was ordered to return to Spain with Louis. He was, apparently, quite willing to comply, under the protection and on the faith of those 'quibus se credere non dubitavit.'[2]

The mission to Hārūnu'l-Rashīd consisted of Sigismund and Lantfrid, together with a certain Jew named Isaac, who was probably appointed as interpreter. It seems to have set out towards the close of 797, and was absent for three years, during which time Sigismund and Lantfrid died, probably after the mission had been accomplished, as Hārūn sent two ambassadors on his return embassy.[3] It is impossible to determine the route they took, whether it lay by way of Egypt through Palestine and Syria, in which case they would pass

[1] The changed attitude of Charles towards Constantinople in 798 seems to be indicated by the increasing favour with which Greek missions appear to be treated. It is interesting to notice that Einhard records, without any apparent disapproval, the blinding of Constantine *propter morum insolentiam,* (no. 11,a. 798), and in this he is in agreement with Mas'ūdī (no. 33, pp. 227-228). For details of the mission, see *Ann. Einhardi, loc. cit.*; Bury, no. 74, p. 317. For the significance of the marriage and the light it throws on Charles's annoyance at his coronation by Leo III on Christmas Day, 800, it may be of interest to notice the place of marriage with the Emperor's widow (cf. Anastasius I, who married Ariadne, the widow of Zeno, in 491, and Nicephorus II, who married Theophano, the widow of Romanus II, in 963) as constituting a valid claim to the succession of the Empire. The marriage of Constantine V with Rotrud (cf. Maurice, the husband of Justin II's daughter, who succeeded in 582) had failed, and either Charles or Irene appears to have suggested the step. On the whole, it is hardly probable that Charles made the proposal, though it was quite in keeping with a certain Teutonic custom which persisted despite the Church's legislation against incest. See the writer's paper 'The Human Khil'at,' no. 68.

[2] See *supra*, p. 20. The sentence is capable of the simple interpretation that to trust Charles was a safer course than to trust the Umayyad Court, but it may be that the inclusion of this sentence in the *Annals* implies something more than a boast of *Franca fides*, and that the confidence implies the regularization of the position of Charles as the protector of Muslim interests in Spain. See *infra*, pp. 32 ff.

[3] *Ann Einhardi*, no. 11, a. 801. This suggestion would to some extent meet Barthold's strictures on the incident. If it is valid, it shows that Lantfrid and Sigismund died on their way back to France (cf. *Khristianski Vostok*, I, 77). He makes a more serious attack, however, in the statement that Hārūn's envoys arrived empty-handed. If his view of the passage is correct, to say the least, it is extraordinary and most unusual. But, as Barthold has so frequently pointed out to his opponents, 'the authorities are silent on the point.' It is clear that the outstanding gift was the elephant, which dwarfed all other gifts. Moreover, there is no evidence that Hārūn's envoys *did* appear before Charles 'empty-handed' nor that they accompanied Isaac all the way.

through Jerusalem, or whether they sailed to Antioch or Beyrut and proceeded by the route through Aleppo, Rakka, and down the Euphrates, in which case they would not touch Jerusalem. On the whole, the latter would seem the more probable solution, as Antioch was the principal port for the overland trade with the East, were it not for the difficulty in accounting for the mission from the Patriarch in 799.[1]

The instructions to the ambassadors are unknown, but the consequences of their success suggest one or more of three possible objectives: first, the regularization of the position of Charles as protector of the 'Abbāsid interests and adherents in Spain and the Western Mediterranean; secondly, an alliance with Hārūnu'l-Rashīd, involving mutual coöperation, Charles against Spain and Hārūn against the Byzantine Empire, or permission for Irene to make peace with the 'Abbāsids; thirdly, to obtain freedom of access and protection of pilgrims visiting the Holy Places in Palestine, particularly Jerusalem, from either Muslim or Greek oppression. The first and second objectives, in so far as they deal with an alliance with the 'Abbāsids, may well have been the objects of Pippin's mission also, as the political situation had not fundamentally changed.[2] The only evidence, as already indicated, is of the nature of deductions from

[1] Joranson rejects the testimony of the *Miracula Sancti Genesii* (no. 107, p. 243, n. 10), which Bréhier (no. 60, p. 281) would admit. In favour of Bréhier's plea, it must be admitted that the customary route would be known to the writer of the *Miracula*, and that whenever the work was written, prior to the Crusades, there would probably be little variation in the route taken, and if it is a late compilation, the existence of some earlier document must be presupposed. The question would still remain, in the light of the paucity of Oriental knowledge of Western affairs, of accounting for the occasion of the mission by some other event. The Patriarch's blessing (*benedictionem*) (*Ann. Reg. Franc*, no. 11, a. 799) requires some such hypothesis.

[2] The change in Irene's attitude towards the West has already been noticed. First of all, there is the attempt to remove the obstacles arising from iconoclasm, culminating in the Council of Constantinople in 787; secondly, the surrender of Beneventum and Istria; and thirdly, the negotiations of marriage, which was opposed in high official circles in Constantinople as inexpedient and may have hastened Irene's downfall. Charles must have been aware of her difficulties and of his own interest in maintaining her in power. Peace with Hārūnu'l-Rashīd would relieve her of considerable embarrassment, but in the event of her overthrow, the revival of hostility between Constantinople and the West would appear to be a certain result, so any change in Byzantine opinion which rested on Irene's efforts can only be regarded as temporary. Cf. Bury, no. 74, pp. 317–321; Barthold, no. 56, p. 272.

later events, and therefore it is very slender, but the position of Charles does appear to have been strengthened in the directions indicated.

First, then, the affairs of Spain. The mere dispatch of the mission appears to have effected some reconciliation in the minds of the northern Muslim rulers on the propriety of handing over cities and districts to the protection of a Christian monarch. Apart from the advance of Alfonso, already a vassal of Charles, as far as Lisbon, there were other developments in which the services of 'Abdu'llāh may have aided the advance of Frankish overlordship. Ḥasan, *walī* of Huesca, sent the keys of the city to Charles in 799, and promised to surrender it to him if opportunity occurred. The element of hesitation indicated by the words *si opportunitas eveniret* can be best interpreted in the light of Sulaimān's difficulties in 778 and the removal of any possibility of their recurrence by a grant of authority by the Khalīfah.[1] Barcelona was captured in 802, after a siege of two years, and an attempt from Cordova to relieve it failed. The relieving force was turned against Alfonso, who received an unexpected check.[2] Zaid, *walī* of Barcelona, visited Louis and made his submission to him.[3] Some time between 802 and 806, there appears to have been a successful attempt on the part of the Umayyads of Cordova to retake Pampeluna, Huesca, and Tarragona, but in the latter year these towns surrendered to Pippin and their *walīs* did homage.[4] It is important, moreover, to notice that, contrary to the general policy of Charles, the cities of the Spanish Mark appear to

---

[1] *Ann. Einhardi*, no. 11, a. 799: 'Et Azan Sarracenus, praefectus Oscae, claves urbis cum aliis donis regi misit, promittens eam se dediturum, si opportunitas eveniret.' Cf. *supra*, p. 20.

[2] *Vita Hlud. Pii*, no. 47, c. 13; Al-Makkārī, no. 29, II, 102.

[3] *Vita Hlud. Pii*, no. 47, cc. 10, 13. Zaid's refusal to admit the troops of Louis in 800 raises the same question as that of Sulaimān of Saragossa in 778 (see *supra*, pp. 11-12), and can be met by the same explanation, since, though his surrender in 802 *may* have been due to the failure of the relief force from Cordova, his previous commendation to Charles at least throws doubt on such a reason, while the authorization of Charles to act as official guardian of 'Abbāsid interests in Spain would at least serve as a pretext, even if it did not supply the motive of his submission. Zaid, however, appears to have been a thoroughly unsatisfactory vassal, as is shown later by his banishment by Charles (*infra*, p. 39). Cf. Abel and Simson, no. 51, II, 257-266; Lembke, no. 113, I, 376 ff.

[4] *Ann. Reg. Franc.*, no. 11, a. 806; Lembke, no. 113, I, 378. For a possible explanation of this outbreak owing to the rebellion of Ibn Shammās, see *supra*, p. 18.

have retained their Muslim governors, and the status of the Mark as a Muslim political unit would account, in part, for the fact that it did not form the basis of the Christian reconquest of Spain.[1] The Moors and Saracens who had attacked and ravaged the Balearic Isles in 798 were defeated in the following year. This attack came, apparently, from Spain.[2] A later attack of the same sort resulted in an authoritative statement of the view of the government of Baghdād as to the sphere of Charles's activity. In 810 and 812 the Moors fell upon Corsica, Sardinia, and Sicily. This attack was followed by a descent upon Italy in the following year, and Charles, apparently, made representations at the court of Khalīfah through Gregory the Patrician, governor of Sicily, with the result that an embassy from the Khalīfah visited Gregory in 813. The results of the embassy are preserved fairly completely in a letter from Leo III to Charles. This letter is important, for it contains the official view of Baghdād, not only on the affairs of Spain but also on the position of the Christian Emperor in the West as the recognized champion and protector of 'Abbāsid interests there. Leo states that, in reply to Gregory's representations as to the futility of making any peace treaty with the Saracens, their ambassadors replied that they refused to answer for the Spanish Muḥammadans, since they were not under the jurisdiction (*dicione* = *wilāyat*) of their kingdom, but they promised to support the efforts of Charles and Gregory in the West. The answer concludes with the words 'Nos a parte nostra, et vos a vestra, a Christianorum finibus eos abiciamus.' After this statement they confirmed the pact for ten years.[3] Although Charles is not specifically

[1] Cf. the position of Aureolus (*infra*, pp. 39 f.). Lavisse and Rambaud, *Histoire générale*, II, 663.

[2] *Ann. Reg. Franc.*, no. 11, a. 798; cf. *ibid.*, a. 809, 'Mauri quoque de Hispania'; and 810, 'Mauri de tota Hispania maxima classe comparata.'

[3] *Ann. Reg. Franc.*, no. 11, a. 810, 812, 813; Jaffé, no. 26, pp. 326–327. It is impossible to decide the year in which the mission was sent. Judging from the length of time taken by previous missions, combined with the fact that the dispatch was addressed to Hārūnu'l-Rashīd, it would seem that the attacks of 810 were the cause of the representations. The delay in the answer may have been due to the civil wars between Al-Amīn and Al-Ma'mūn. Barthold, in his reply to Vasiliev (no. 56, pp. 267 f.), attacks Weil's assertion that Frankish intervention prevented an attack on the 'Abbāsids by the Spanish Umayyads (no. 134, II, 76) with the remark, 'What the Spanish Umayyads could do Weil does not explain.' It is suggested that the maritime warfare and piracy of the Spanish Moors (Mauri), which produced the agreement of this year (813), is sufficient answer to the query.

mentioned in this passage, it is clear, from an earlier remark in the letter, that Gregory was acting for him, and his area of authority would be implied in 'non sub dicione regni nostri.'[1] The sentence quoted clearly indicates a sphere of activity handed over to Charles, and it seems almost certain that Charles was recognized as the representative of the Khalīfah in the West. His constitutional and diplomatic relationship belongs to a later part of this essay. This conjecture, moreover, receives some support from evidence unearthed by Vasiliev. In 1888 Jamīl Nakhlī Mudawwar printed in Cairo a work entitled *Hadārat al-Islām fī dāri'l-salām*—'Muslim culture in Baghdād,'—wherein there are several letters from the son of one of the nobles of Khurasān, giving a picture of the life of the Caliphate in the time of Hārūn. In 186 A.H. (= 802 A.D.), the story-teller went as head of an embassy directed against the Spanish Umayyads. He took a number of presents, including a large white elephant, formerly owned by the Khalīfah Al-Mahdī, to whom it was sent by an Indian *rājā*. The route he took was from Baghdād, through Kūfa, into Syria, sailing from Beyrut to Malta, whence he sailed to Marseilles and so to Rome. There he was admitted by Charles and held a conversation on the subject of the Spanish Umayyads. He returned by way of Tunis, Alexandria, and Cairo, and thence performed the *Ḥajj*, meeting Hārūn in Arabia.[2]

[1] Leo states that this letter is a reply to one from Charles, which Leo had sent to Gregory of Sicily (Jaffé, no. 26, p. 325). The reference to Hārūnu'l-Rashīd's successor ('qui fuit servus,' etc.) appears to be an allusion to Al-Ma'mūn, who was the son of a Persian slave (Muir, no. 120, p. 475) and had received the allegiance of the Holy Places of Arabia by August, 812 (*ibid*., pp. 490–492), rather than to Al-Amīn (as Jaffé, no. 26, p. 326, n. 3, supposes). In the reply of the Saracen *missi* occurs the curious word *relictus*, which may well be a literal translation of the word *khalīfah*. Moreover, the policy and struggle of the Ma'mūn suits the sentence 'Sed ecce nunc, postquam omnia quae pater suus habuit sibi subiecit, vult firma stabilitate hoc, quod petimus, pactum servare.' The concluding passage in which he defines the position of Charles is as follows: 'De Spanis autem non spondimus; quia non sunt sub dicione regni nostri. Sed in quantum valemus eos superare, sicut vos ita et nos contra illos in mare dimicare promittimus; etsi soli nos non valemus. Nos a parte nostra, et vos a vestra, a Christianorum finibus abiciamus.' The whole passage throws an interesting light on the mission from Ma'mūn in 831 (see *infra*, pp. 37, 40 and n. 4), and the possible influence of the mission on Einhard's references in the *Vita Caroli Magni*, if that work was written between 831 and 836, as Halphen suggests (no. 97, pp. 98–103).

[2] Vasiliev, no. 132, pp. 69–70. For the importance of Jamīl Nakhlī and a brief summary of the work, see V. Krachkovsky, 'The Historical Novel in Contemporary Arabic Literature' (in Russian), *Journ. Min. Pub. Instr.*, June, 1911, pp. 271–273. Vasiliev used the second edition

Secondly, owing to the almost continuous state of hostility existing between Constantinople and Baghdād, it is difficult to base any argument of a Franco-'Abbāsid alliance on any isolated expedition.[1] Further, the submission of Irene in 798 to the Khalīfah's demands for tribute and the acceptance of her submission by Hārūnu'l-Rashīd are not strong evidence for the intervention of the embassy in the interests of peace, although at the time of the Byzantine mission to Charles, it may have been a vital issue. On the other hand, it is barely conceivable that the mission arrived in time to lend any influence to the acceptance of the proffered submission.[2] Moreover, the fresh outbreak of hostilities following the overthrow of Irene can be accounted for on other grounds. The letter of Nicephorus I to Hārūnu'l-Rashīd in December, 802, declining to pay the tribute, is sufficient explanation.[3] There remains, however, the letter of Hadrian to Charles, to which reference has already been made. It is true that this letter was already fifteen or sixteen years old, and that it contains no direct suggestion of such an alliance, but there is no reason for supposing that it was altogether forgotten, or that the indirect suggestion was entirely missed.[4] Further, such a suggestion may well have come from 'Abdu'llāh in 797, when he saw the Rūmī (Byzantine) ambassadors at the court of Charles. In addition, the proposals of peace sent by Nicephorus to Charles in 803 suggest that the Byzantine government may have suspected the existence of some alliance, or at least of a friendly understanding, between Aachen and Baghdād.[5] These negotiations broke down, ostensibly, on the de-

of Jamīl Nakhlī's work (Cairo, 1905), pp. 265-328. The work is really a historical novel but Vasiliev states that 'it is written in the form of a serious historical work, with references to Arabic sources.' Barthold states in his reply to Vasiliev that he 'does not show in what respect Pippin (and, it follows, Charles too) was strengthened by the alliance' (no. 56, p. 267). The statement given in the text (*supra*) shows the possible effects of such recognition, and supports Abel's suggestion that the lack of results in 768 was due to the death of Pippin (no. 51, I, 232).

[1] The situation in 797 differed somewhat from that of 765, as has been shown already, cf. *supra*, p. 10. But under Pippin there can be no doubt that the objective was the distraction of Constantine (cf. *Camb. Med. Hist.*, no. 78, IV, 18, for the danger), and though there is no evidence to connect the outbreak of hostilities in 766 (*ibid.*, pp. 122-123) with the mission, Al-Manṣūr's action may quite conceivably have been due to its influence.

[2] Theophanes, no. 45, p. 473; Weil, no. 134, II, 157; Bury, no. 74, p. 249.
[3] Weil, no. 134, II, 159; Abū'l-Faraj, no. 2, p. 151; Brooks, no. 64, XV, 743.
[4] See *supra*, pp. 15-16.
[5] *Ann. Reg. Franc.*, no. 11, a. 803; *Ann. Fuld.*, no. 6, a. 803.

mand of Charles to be recognized as the Emperor of the West, a condition unacceptable to the East, and Nicephorus does not appear to have answered Charles's missive.[1] The immediate conclusion of peace with Hārūnu'l-Rashīd in 804, however, does appear to be connected with the breakdown of diplomatic relations with the West, as the terms of peace were identical with those granted to Irene in 798, namely, the payment of tribute.[2] This peace, however, was short-lived. The next two years were marked by raids by Hārūn into Byzantine territory, while the Western relations of the Empire culminated in somewhat languid hostilities with Charles over the question of Venice and Dalmatia.[3] The double attack may have been due to the realization of Nicephorus that some compact existed between Charles and Hārūn, and it would seem that he realized further that his main hope of peace on the eastern frontier and security at home rested on the dissolution of the compact. The *Annales Regni Francorum*[4] mention the dispatch of the Byzantine fleet to Dalmatia and state that the last embassy of Charles to Hārūn succeeded in eluding the fleet. The fact that both are recorded in the same passage suggests some association in the mind of the Annalist of the objectives of the fleet and the mission. The failure to break up the friendly understanding ultimately forced Nicephorus to recognize Charles in his new status as Emperor.

The third object appears to have been the provision of safe access to the Holy Places for Christian pilgrims from the West.[5] Before examining the evidence immediately bearing on this subject, it is necessary to make some estimate of the situation in Jerusalem. The Christians do not appear to have suffered an exceptionally hard lot at the hands of the Muslim authorities, either there or at Antioch or at Alexandria, until Nicephorus broke the peace in 802. There seems

[1] Bury, no. 74, p. 321.

[2] *Camb. Med. Hist.*, no. 78, IV, 125–126; Bury, no. 74, p. 250; Abū'l-Faraj, no. 1, a. 804; Michael Syrus, no. 36, bk. xii, cap. 3, 1.

[3] Bury, no. 74, pp. 323 ff.

[4] *Ann. Reg. Franc.*, no. 11, a. 806, 'Classis a Niciforo imperatore, cui Niceta patricius praeerat, ad reciperandam Dalmatiam mittitur; et legati, qui dudum ante quattuor fere annos ad regem Persarum missi sunt, per ipsas Grecarum navium stationes transvecti ad Tarvisiani portus receptaculum, nullo adversariorum sentiente, regressi sunt.'

[5] Cf. *supra*, p. 8, n. 3. For a discussion of the state of the Christians in Palestine see Kleinclausz, no. 109, pp. 213–217, 222, 225–226; Bréhier, no. 60, pp. 278–281.

to have been at all times a considerable number of Christians in all ranks of office throughout the 'Abbāsid period, a fact attested by the continuous, and apparently useless, proclamations against their employment.[1] This fact is of interest in relation to the relations of Charles with that dynasty. The orthodox party of Alexandria captured the patriarchate by means of Muslim aid, and the Patriarch of Antioch contemporary with Cosmas appears to have been in close touch with official circles.[2] Moreover, during the reign of Constantine Copronymus and his successors, there appears to have existed a general feeling that the image-worshipping Christians had a greater hope of fair treatment from the Muslim than from the heretical Greek.[3] The iconoclastic controversy, followed by the *filioque* dispute, had, in fact, alienated from Constantinople not only the West, but also the East, driving together the four Apostolic sees of Rome, Alexandria, Antioch, and Jerusalem.[4] In considering the aim of any 'protectorate,' therefore, it is necessary that the possibility of its objectives being anti-Greek as well as anti-Muslim should be borne in mind. The incident would then be the exact parallel, if not the antetype, of the French claim of 1850 in face of Russian pretensions. Accordingly, if the motive of the request happened to be or to contain the object of the elimination of Byzantine influence in Jerusalem, then its presentation would be facilitated and Hārūn's acquiescence and grant would not be strange.[5] Further, if Charles aimed at excluding Byzantines from the favour of the 'Abbāsids, some step of the sort would be necessary for the official representa-

[1] Cf. Arnold, no. 52, pp. 75–88.

[2] Eutychius, no. 18, II, 384–386; Theophanes, no. 45, p. 669; Michael Syrus, no. 36, II, 511.

[3] On the hostility of the Oriental Christians (Hefele-LeClercq, no. 102, pp. 714–725) to the Isaurians see Michael Syrus, *loc. cit. supra*, p. 8, n. 3.

[4] Cf. Council of 763 and letter of Cosmas. See *supra*, pp. 7–8.

[5] This reason would be sufficient to account for Hārūnu'l-Rashīd's spontaneous (?) gift of *potestas* (*wilāyat* or *ḥukūmat*) over Jerusalem and the Holy Places. The Anonymous Monk of Saint Gall appears to have had access to some first-hand account in the speech he ascribes to the Khalīfah (Jaffé, no. 26, p. 678), and the main difficulties of interpretation seem to arise from the failure to recognize that the speech is from the overlord to his vassal's representative. Bréhier goes astray in translating *potestati* as *propriété*; its correct translation (cf. Poeta Saxo, no. 40, p. 596) would appear to be *dicioni* (*wilāyat* or *ḥukūmat, ut supra*), that is, authority or jurisdiction of a subordinate order. The *advocatus* corresponds to the *wasīlah* or *wakīl* of a major vassal at court. It is suggested, with due respect to Halphen, that the speech corresponds too closely to the forms of Oriental court practice to be set aside lightly as mere invention.

tion of the interests of the Christians of Jerusalem in 'Abbāsid court circles. The work would be carried out by a deputy (*wakīl*) and the personal presence of Charles would be in no way necessary.[1] In the West, on the other hand, it would bear a double interpretation—the protection of Catholics against the persecutions of a heretical Emperor, and the protection of Christians against Muslim oppression.[2]

The Annals, however, appear to leave little room to doubt that there was some transaction of the nature of a transfer to Charles of some form of authority over Jerusalem. In 799, a monk who had been sent by the Patriarch of Jerusalem arrived at Aachen with the blessing of the Patriarch and relics of the place of the Resurrection. It is reasonable to suppose that the cause of his coming was either a visit to Jerusalem by the mission from Charles on its way to Hārūnu' l-Rashīd or news of that mission's journey to Baghdād. At any rate, this is chronologically possible, if the time taken by the priest Zacharias to go to Jerusalem and return is any guide.[3] Further, if both of these possibilities are ruled out, there still remains the question as to the cause or reason of the dispatch of the mission by the Patriarch. The only remaining possibility would seem to be thanks for the alms which, according to Einhard, Charles was in the habit of sending to the Christians in Syria, Jerusalem, and elsewhere. On his return, the monk was escorted by Zacharias, who returned to Rome on the first of December in the following year with two monks, whom the Patriarch had sent, bearing not only the keys of the Church of the Holy Sepulchre, but also the keys of the city and a banner. It should be noticed that these offerings were of two distinct classes; the gift of the keys of the Church constituted an ecclesi-

[1] Such grants of authority or revenues of territories to prominent officials who could not expect nor were expected to be present in person to perform the functions of government are common enough in Muslim history. The *wakīl* in this case was to be Hārūnu'l-Rashīd himself ('et ego advocatus [*wakīl*] eius ero super eam,' Jaffé, no. 26, p. 678). The assumption that Hārūn wished to eliminate Byzantine influence in Palestine is supported by the evidence of Barthold (no. 56, pp. 284 ff.) and satisfies his objection.

[2] Hence probably the rise of the crusading legends of Charles and later claims of France to jurisdiction in Syria and Palestine; cf. Rauschen, no. 126, pp. 45 ff., 141 ff.; Viard, no. 46, III, 160–177; Kleinclausz, no. 109, pp. 228–233; Hartmann, no. 101, esp. pp. 41, 45. The writer desires to take this opportunity of acknowledging the kindness of Professor James Westfall Thompson of Chicago for calling his attention to the articles of Kleinclausz and Hartmann.

[3] See the opposing views of Joranson (no. 107, pp. 248–249) and Bréhier (no. 60, p. 282).

astical gesture on the part of the Patriarch, and it would lie within his rights; the keys of the city[1] and the banner,[2] however, belonged to the realm of politics, and their surrender could not have been made without definite orders from the Khalīfah or his Syrian viceroy. The impression at the Frankish court certainly appears to have been that Charles had gained some degree of control over the affairs of Jerusalem. Both Einhard, in the *Vita Caroli Magni*,[3] and later the *Poeta Saxo* in the following lines seem to suggest this.

'Ascribique locum sanctum Hierosolimorum
Concessit propriae Caroli semper dicioni.'[4]

These statements, combined with the gift of robes of honour (*vestes*), seem to indicate the appointment of Charles to some position in the 'Abbāsid hierarchy, and that position would appear to be the office of *walī* (*praepositus*) of Jerusalem.[5] The action of the Patriarch, who

[1] Joranson, following the suggestion of Halphen (no. 15, p. 48, n. 1), appears to be wrong in his attack on Bréhier's interpretation of the Patriarch's surrender of the keys of the city to Charles. Nor is he accurate in limiting the grounds of the inference to analogy with the Bishop of Rome. The year 799 (*Ann. Einhardi*, no. 11,)supplies an instance from the Muslim world: 'et Azan Sarracenus, praefectus Oscae, claves urbis cum aliis donis regi misit, promittens eam se dediturum, si opportunitas eveniret.' This instance seems to be conclusive. The question of the text of the *Ann. Laur. Min.*, however, remains. Bréhier replies (no. 60, pp. 282-285) to Joranson and argues strongly for their validity against Joranson's view that the words 'claves etiam civitatis et montis' are a gloss or later addition. The assumption that they were added, however, would not finally dispose of their validity as evidence. Joranson (p. 249) appears to make too much of *benedictionis causa* as a difficulty. The phrase appears to apply to the relics, and the Patriarch's blessing on Charles would, in the circumstances, be hardly out of place.

[2] Kleinclausz (no. 109, pp. 217-218, n. 2), following a gloss, regards *vexillum* as a processional crucifix. The evidence seems to be weak and the attempt to use it suggests special pleading. If the account of *Ann. Laur. Maiores*, 'claves etiam civitatis et montis cum vexillo' (*M.G.H.*, SS., I, 188), is allowed at all, the *vexillum* from its position would appear to be one of the political insignia, i.e., an 'Abbāsid *vexillum*.

[3] Einhard, no. 15, p. 46 (c. 16). '[Aaron] non solum quae petebantur fieri permisit sed etiam sacrum illum et salutarem locum ut illius potestati adscriberetur concessit.' Granting Halphen's contention of the late date of the composition of this work, this statement would still remain valid as evidence of the impression produced on Einhard's mind that Jerusalem was placed within Charles's jurisdiction. The passage, if composed after Mā'mūn's embassy in 831, might quite conceivably reflect the confirmation of the grant by Hārūnu'l-Rashīd's successor, who 'vult firma stabilitate hoc, quod petimus, pactum servare.' Cf. Jaffé, no. 26, p. 325, and *supra*, p. 28 and n. 5. If so, then Halphen's attack on Bréhier would recoil on his own argument.

[4] *Poeta Saxo*, no. 40, p. 596 (bk. iv, vv. 90-91), following the passage of Einhard cited above, n. 3.

[5] See *infra*, pp. 35 f.

would be his principal and most imposing vassal, points to the same conclusion. But it must not be forgotten that the action implied the suzerainty of Hārūn over Charles, to whom he stood in exactly the same relation as Charles to Ḥasan, *walī* of Huesca. The solution to the problem lies not in the terminology or theory of international law, but in Oriental feudal law of the early Middle Ages.[1] In 801 Isaac the Jew, the sole survivor of the original embassy, returned, preceded by two ambassadors from Hārūnu'l-Rashīd. Lantfrid and Sigismund had died on the way. Hārūn had sent a Persian and the governor of Egypt, Ibrahīm ibnu'l-Aghlab, bearing rich presents,

'gemmas, aurum, vestes et aromata crebro
Ac reliquias orientis opes direxerat illi,'

as well as the famous elephant, Abū'l-'Abbās.[2]

[1] The use of the terms 'protection' and 'protectorate' in this connection, as in many others, is unfortunate, owing to the technical implication of an independent overlordship of a paramount power which has arisen in modern times. One thing is perfectly clear, viz., that Hārūnu'l-Rashīd would never have tolerated the erection of a 'Frankish protectorate' over any of his dominions, any more than Shah 'Alam II, in 1803, would admit his submission to a 'British protectorate.' (See the writer's paper 'The Political Theory of the Indian Mutiny, no. 71, pp. 77–91). This fact, however, does not rule out of possibility the genuineness of the records or any transaction, but it forces the recognition of a subordinate status within the 'Abbāsid Caliphate. The former position (of a 'protectorate') Bréhier has abandoned (no. 60, p. 278), but his attempt (*ibid.*, p. 287) to solve his difficulty by a resort to a vague expression of 'un pouvoir, notion large et un peu vague qui indique surtout une autorité morale' is no more fortunate. The claim of the authorities that Charles was granted *potestas* implies a definite authority, and the word can only be regarded as a technical political term. The interplay of claims to overlordship is not confined to the East, and it can hardly be dismissed on grounds of improbability in the face of Carlyle's account of the relations of Æthelstan and Hakon (no. 79, pp. 7–8; cf., too, *infra*, pp. 33–34).

[2] *Ann Laur. Min.*, no. 7, a. 801; Poeta Saxo, no. 40, p. 596. The ambassadors of Hārūnu'l-Rashīd appear to have arrived at the beginning of May, and Isaac in October. The fact that Hārūnu'l-Rashīd sent two ambassadors seems to indicate the probability that both Lantfrid and Sigismund reached Baghdād as noticed above. On the elephant see Appendix III.

III

THE STATUS OF CHARLES THE GREAT

AT this point it is appropriate to examine the political implications of the gifts and transactions, and the evidence available for the interpretation.

An initial error can be removed at once, the error of regarding the relations between Hārūnu'l-Rashīd and Charles as an alliance in the modern sense of the word. It is not so in early Muslim relations. Hārūnu'l-Rashīd regarded himself quite as much the successor of the kings of Persia as the successor of the Prophet, and the king of Persia was the King of Kings and the shadow of God on earth.[1] To him all other kings were vassals; from him they derived their royal estate. Where he could not be in person, there they were as his deputies. The bond which bound together the king and his deputy was the bond of love or friendship. These terms never implied equality but always—as in Anglo-Saxon—the relation of the protector to the protected, and *vice versa*. Now it is known that Hārūnu'l-Rashīd and his predecessors regarded the Emperors at Constantinople as their vassals and tributaries.[2] It is hardly probable that Hārūn would re-

[1] For a fuller statement see the writer's paper, 'The Oriental Despot,' no. 67, also Goldziher, no. 96.

[2] The historian Ibnu'l Ṭiqṭaqā, writing early in the fourteenth century in praise of Mongol rule, spares no pains to show the superiority of their power over the power of their predecessors. He can be acquitted, therefore, of any bias in favour of either Umayyad or 'Abbāsid. After stating that 'the Umayyad empire was very great but it was not to be compared with that enjoyed by the Mongol princes,' he proceeds as follows: 'As much can be said of the 'Abbāsids. From this point of view they never equalled the power attained by the Mongol princes, although the empire remained in their family for five hundred years, and the extent of their empire was such that they drew tribute from the greater part of the world. . . . Certainly in the days of Rashīd, the revenues of the world were gathered into a single [*lit.* combined] account, as the histories of the period testify. The first of these Khalīfahs, Al-Manṣūr, Al-Mahdī, Al-Rashīd, Al-Ma'mūn . . . drew revenues from a great part of the world and their power was most imposing. Despite this fact, their empire was not free from weakness and debility from many points of view. Rūm [the Byzantine Empire], for example, was never obedient to them and no year passed in which these Khalīfahs were not compelled to renew the war with the Christian kings of that state. Despite that, they still had difficulty in collecting from them the tribute they had imposed and these kings [the Byzantine emperors] continued

gard Charles in any other light. But there is even stronger evidence for the conception in the terminology of the *Poeta Saxo*. He brings out two points very clearly. In the account of the year 801 he says that Hārūn

'curaverat ultro
Eius amicitias se foedere iungere firmo';[1]

and on the mission of 807, he also states

'Persarum princeps illi devinctus amore
Precipuo fuerat, nomen habens Aaron;
Gratia cui Caroli prae cunctis regibus atque
Illo principibus tempore cara fuit.'[2]

The words *amor* and *amicitia* are technical terms, indicating a closer relation than mere alliance. Further, *precipuo amore* represents a clearly defined position. That vassal is *devinctus amore precipuo* who is one of the king's friends, and as such eats at the king's table and receives his robes of honour direct from the king. The evidence of Xenophon on the habit of Cyrus of feasting his friends and giving robes to them is clearly a parallel case. The bond of friendship with Charles, then, placed him in the inner circle of Hārūn's chief vassals.[3]

Secondly, the ritual of incorporation into the king's body, which is the status of the 'friend,' is the bestowal of a robe of honour by the lord. This robe derives its honour not from the richness of its texture but from the fact that it has been worn by the king, or donor, and has been taken off—hence the Arabic term, the *khil'at*—and passed on to the vassal or friend—hence the Hebrew term *hălīpōt smālūt*, a

---

to refuse to obey.' (Ibnu'l-Ṭiqṭaqā, no. 23a, pp. 38–39; no. 23b, pp. 47–48.) The pretensions to suzerainty are clear, and the annual wars with the continued insistence on tribute as the sole condition of peace are amply supported in other places. Moreover, the wars themselves are evidence both of the 'Abbāsids' claims and of their intention to enforce them.

[1] Poeta Saxo, no. 40, p. 596 (bk. iv, vv. 83–84).

[2] *Ibid.*, p. 615, bk. v, vv. 307–310. Cf. Einhard, no. 15, c. 16; 'Cum Aaron ... talem habuit in amicitia concordiam ut is gratiam eius omnium qui in toto orbe terrarum erant regum ac principum amicitiae praeponerat ...,' and Monachus Sangallensis, no. 38, pp. 677–678 (bk. ii, c. 9).

[3] Both among the Germans and in the East the idea of *friendship* implies the relation of protector to the protected and *vice versa*, and it does not appear to be used of equals. Cf. Bosworth and Toller, *Anglo-Saxon Dictionary*, *s. v. wine*, and the writer's notes, no. 70, pp. 597, n. 1, 600, n. 4; also Xenophon, no. 49, i, 71 (bk. i, c. 4, sect. 26); ii, 3 (bk. v, c. 1, sect. 2).

garment to be passed on. In this case the delegation of authority was made for a particular or special purpose, or if the bestowal was to denote special honour or distinction, the king, like Cyrus in the case of Araspas, took off the garment he was wearing and bestowed it on the vassal. This was technically known as a *malbūs khās*—*vestis praecipua*, a special robe—and the man was one of the king's friends.[1] The gift of robes to Charles, then, implied the proclamation of overlordship over him, and his acceptance implied the acknowledgement of that suzerainty.[2] This fact accounts for a curious passage in the account of the Monk of Saint Gall. Charles may have realized the position involved, as in Germanic language *friend* and *friendship* have the same significance. This is doubtful, however, and the gift of Frisian *pallia* in 807 need only be taken as an attempt to repay a compliment in kind, except in so far as it establishes beyond any doubt the gift of robes of honour to Charles by Hārūnu'l-Rashīd.[3]

Now it happens that in Māwardī's work on the constitution of the Caliphate, *al-Aḥkāmu'l-sulṭāniyyah*, written in the middle of the eleventh century of our era, there is provision for such a status as that described, namely the *imārat* of conquest, which is sharply distinguished from the ordinary forms of that office by the fact that it lies outside the free choice of the Khalīfah and that it may devolve on a non-Muslim. Consequently the conditions of recognition and

---

[1] See the writer's paper, 'Two instances of *Khil'at* in the Bible,' no. 69, and 'The Oriental Despot,' no. 67, pp. 240 ff., 245.

[2] Cf. Manucci, no. 30, II, 43–44: '... the envoys of Balkh began to talk of a return to their own country, Aurungzēb, at their leave-taking, ordered them to receive two sets of robes of rich stuff for each man, ... for the King of Balkh he sent as a remembrance ... nine costly and beautiful sets of robes, with the whole of which the envoys were much satisfied. Ignorance thus made them satisfied, for they were not aware that the King of the Moguls sends *sarāpās* (sets of robes) to subjects only. To send a *sarāpā* to any one is to declare him to be a subject. If he submit to this, no further present need be added.'

The Mughal system of government appears to have been derived, ultimately, from the 'Abbāsid system. Sarkar, no. 130, p. 8.

A horse or elephant from the king's stable was not infrequently added to the dresses which composed the gift of *khil'at*. It may be presumed that the animal had, theoretically at least, been ridden by the donor, so it too was of the nature of a *khil'at*. So Grant Duff, no. 85, I, 406, n. 1. His attempt to distinguish between the *sarāpā* and the *khil'at* on this basis, however, cannot be maintained. See Appendix III.

[3] Monachus Sangallensis, no. 38, p. 677 (bk. ii, c. 9).

investiture include strict terms to safeguard the interests of the Faithful. The situation he describes is as follows: When a chief has made himself master of the country by force of victorious arms, he is invested with the office of *amīr* by the Khalīfah, who intrusts to him the government of the country and all those functions that are characteristic of the office of the *amīr*. This condition naturally excludes the function of the *imāmat*, the leadership in prayer, and so protects the religious interests of his Muslim subjects. Apart from this, however, he obtains by the Khalīfah's delegation of authority a legal sanction which remedies the defects otherwise inherent in his status, so that what was before forbidden (to the Muslimīn) now is permitted. Provided, then, he observes the conditions noticed above, when he has been recognized and invested by the Khalīfah, his authority is valid and resistance to his command is illegal.[1] Māwardī wrote when the Caliphate was 'at the lowest ebb of its degradation, and the theoretical character of his account of it is in striking contrast to the actual historic facts of the case'.[2] It is not in this respect, however, that his main significance lies, though the fact that the degradation acted as a stimulus to impel him to turn to history for theoretical support of the authority which in fact no longer existed is important, as implying that even in the golden past theory may have had at times to bow to the facts of the case. Of greater significance, however, is the fact that Māwardī belonged to the school of Shāfi'ī, who began to lecture in Baghdād the year after the death of Hārūnu'l-Rashīd and died in the year 820. For the purposes of this question, therefore, he represents contemporary legal opinion. The position of Charles corresponds so closely with that of the *amīr* described by Māwardī that it would seem that the principles of Muslim constitutional law involved are the same.[3]

The status of Charles, then, would appear to be that of *amīr* of Spain and *walī* of Jerusalem under the 'Abbāsid Khalīfah. In the former capacity he would be the successor of Pippin I and 'Alā ibn Mughīth. As the approved deputy of the Khalīfah, the pious

---

[1] Māwardī, no. 34, pp. 54–57; no. 35, pp. 66–70.
[2] Arnold, no. 54, p. 70.
[3] For the position of Shāfi'ī, see Goldziher, no. 95, p. 53; MacDonald, no. 115, pp. 104 ff.; on Māwardī, see Arnold, *loc. cit.*; Fagnan, no. 88, introduction.

Muslimīn could accept him within their gates without any qualms of conscience. As the *walī* of Jerusalem, it would be proper for him to receive the homage of the Patriarch, while his position would form a diplomatic precedent for Frederick II. If this analysis be correct, in the year 801 Hārūn's triumphs exceeded those of Alexander the Great, for he was lord, not only of the Muslim world, including a large part of Spain,[1] but also of the Roman Empire, for in 798 Irene had again acknowledged the tributary status which had dated from 782,[2] and Charles had accepted his overlordship.

In 802 Charles sent another mission to Baghdād. Its return in 806 is noteworthy for the fact that it passed undetected through the Byzantine fleet and landed safely at Treviso.[3] The Eastern fleet, led by the patrician Nicetas, had been sent to recover Dalmatia, and returned the following year after peace had been made with Pippin, king of Italy.[4] Of the mission, Radbert had died on the way back, and Hārūnu'l Rashīd's only envoy appears to have been a certain Persian named 'Abdu'llāh.[5] The Patriarch Thomas of Jerusalem appears to have sent two monks, one named Felix, the other a German, Egilbald, who had changed his name to George and was abbot of the monastery on Mount Olivet.[6] Both missions brought presents; the Patriarch sent relics and the Khalīfah, among many other things, sent a tent[7] and 'pallia sirica multa et preciosa.'[8] The legates were dismissed with honour to Italy, there to await provisions for their return journey. The account of Radbert's mission is recorded with

[1] I.e., at least that part of Spain under the protection of Charles and his vassals; but probably the whole was claimed as subordinate to him. The remark of Einhard that Hārūnu'l-Rashīd was lord of the whole Orient *excepta India* receives an interesting comment in the attempts to conquer India under the early 'Abbāsids. See Muir, no. 120, pp. 441, 471; Murgotten, no. 39, pp. 230 ff.; Smith, no. 131, pp. 363–364.

[2] *Camb. Med. Hist.*, no. 78, IV, 124.

[3] *Ann. Reg. Franc.*, no. 11, a. 806, *cit. supra*, p. 27, n. 4.

[4] *Ibid.*, and Bury, no. 74, pp. 323–324.

[5] *Ann. Reg. Franc.*, no. 11, a. 807. 'Radbertus, missus imperatoris, qui de oriente revertebatur, defunctus est, et legatus regis Persarum nomine Abdella cum monachis de Hierusalem, qui legatione Thomae patriarchae fungebantur, quorum nomina fuere Georgius et Felix, ad imperatorem pervenerunt munera deferentes, quae praedictus rex imperatori miserat.'

[6] *Ann. Reg. Franc.*, no. 11, a. 807.

[7] 'Tentoria atrii mirae magnitudinis et pulchritudinis.' It may be pertinent to suggest the possibility of tent-right. Cf. Huart, no. 103, I, 19.

[8] On *sirica* cf. Procopius, no. 42, p. 193 (bk. i, c. 20, sect. 9, and note).

Status of Charles the Great

some detail by the Monk of Saint Gall, and, as already noticed, the story bears traces of a genuine authority amid its mass of fiction.[1] One other embassy appears to have been sent in 807 by Charles, who addressed his communications to Hārūnu'l-Rashīd. Hārūn died two years later, and the reply which came through Gregory of Sicily in 813 appears to have been sent by Al-Mā'mūn (813–833). Allusion has already been made to it.[2]

The situation, however, was changing rapidly, and Charles had less need of 'Abbāsid support against the Byzantine Empire. The expedition of Nicetas in 806 was its last serious demonstration against the West, and even that appears to have been only half-hearted in its hostility. Charles used for his own ends the revolt of the duke of Venice from Constantinople in 804. Pippin concluded a truce with the Byzantines until 808. Their naval demonstration under Paulus in the following year proved a fiasco, and the departure of their fleet enabled Pippin to subdue Venice in 810. Dalmatia was only saved from the young king's victorious course by the reappearance of Paulus.[3] That year Nicephorus sent Arsaphius to treat with Charles; and at Aachen in 812 the ambassadors of Michael I saluted Charles as Emperor, *Basileus*.[4] The treaty of friendship was signed by Charles at that time, while Michael's signature reached Aachen just after the death of Charles in 814.[5]

The 'Abbāsids also appear to have obtained some degree of satisfaction. The renunciation of Irene's treaty by Nicephorus in 803 had been short-lived. Since he failed to obtain any support from the West, a concerted attack in 804 by the forces of the Caliphate reduced him once more to the status of a tributary. He also promised not to rebuild any dismantled fortresses.[6] While Hārūnu'l-Rashīd was occupied with the affairs of Persia in the following year, he heard that Nicephorus had attacked Cilicia in defiance of the treaty, had captured Tarsus and made prisoners of its garrison.[7] The attack

---

[1] See *supra*, p. 28, n. 5
[2] Jaffé, no. 26, p. 326. See *supra*, p. 25.
[3] Bury, no. 74, pp. 323 ff.
[4] *Ann. Reg. Franc.*, no. 11, a. 811–812; Jaffé, no. 26, pp. 415–416; Bury, no. 74, pp. 324–326.
[5] *Ann. Reg. Franc.*, no. 11, a. 814.
[6] *Camb. Med. Hist.*, no. 78, IV, 126; Bury, no. 74, p. 251. Cf. Mas'ūdī, no. 33, pp. 227–228.
[7] *Camb. Med. Hist.*, no. 78, IV, 126–127.

of Hārūnu'l-Rashīd on the Empire in 806 may quite conceivably have been connected with the return mission of that year to Charles, and it would also account for the readiness of the Byzantine authorities to treat with Charles on the subject of his recognition as Emperor. Since the arms of Nicephorus were fully occupied by an attack of the Bulgarians, and he had no alternative but to submit, he sent a mission to Hārūn requesting peace and renewing the tribute. His subsequent attempt to take advantage of the retirement of the Muslim forces by rebuilding the dismantled forts was thwarted by the unexpected return of the Khalīfah.[1] As a penalty Hārūn seized Thebasa. Hostilities continued throughout the year 807, at first favourably to the Byzantine forces. They appear, however, to have been ejected ultimately from Cilicia, where Harthama was left by Hārūn to rebuild the fortress of Tarsus.[2] An exchange of prisoners in 808, implying a restoration of peace on the old basis, marks the end of Hārūn's dealings with Nicephorus, for he was otherwise occupied until his death in 809.[3] So in the last years of his life he was able to regard himself, in virtue of his military successes over the Byzantine Empire and his diplomatic success with Charles the Great, as Lord of the Two Worlds, the true successor of Alexander the Great.[4]

There remains the question of the affairs of Spain. In 799, Ḥasan, *walī* of Huesca, of his own free will sent the keys of the city to Charles, who dispatched Louis both to take possession of the place and to recapture Barcelona.[5] Barcelona was still under the command of Zaid, who had sworn allegiance to Charles in 797, but he appears to have repented of his act and to have reverted to his allegiance to Cordova. After two years of intermittent siege, Barcelona, on seeing that the Franks were preparing to winter in Spain, surrendered in 801, and Zaid was handed over to Louis, who sent him to Charles.

---

[1] Theophanes, no. 45, p. 482; Brooks, no. 64, xv, 746; *Camb. Med. Hist.*, no. 78, IV, 126.

[2] *Camb. Med. Hist.*, no. 78, IV, 127.

[3] Mas'ūdī, no. 33, pp. 228, 443–444; *Camb. Med. Hist.*, no. 78, IV, 127.

[4] For the place of Alexander the Great in the history and ideas of Oriental monarchy, see Browne, no. 65, I, 118–121, 304–305; II, *passim*; the writer's article 'A New Interpretation of Akbar's "Infallibility" Decree of 1579,' no. 70, p. 594 and n. 2; cf. L. Halphen, no. 97, p. 126, n. 7. 'Alī Ṭabarī's exegesis of Jeremiah, xlix, 35–38 (no. 5, pp. 107–108), appears to be conclusive evidence of the 'Abbāsids' view of their own achievement.

[5] *Ann. Reg. Franc.*, no. 11, a. 799.

He sentenced Zaid to exile.¹ The army of relief sent from Cordova had been checked by William of Toulouse and deflected to Asturias, where Alfonso met with an unexpected defeat.² In the next four years there appears to have been little activity in the Spanish Mark, which was in 805 included in the kingdom of Aquitaine under Louis. In that year Navarre and Pampeluna, having succeeded in throwing off the suzerainty of Cordova, accepted the overlordship and protection of Charles.³ In the meantime, naval preparations had been made for a wholesale attack on the Christian territories in the Mediterranean. The Mauri, probably North African pirates in the employment of Cordova, started a series of attacks on Corsica, Sardinia and Sicily, and Italy. The discovery of the fact that the headquarters of the fleet was in Spain may have been the cause of the campaign of the Franks against Tortosa, at the mouth of the Ebro.⁴ This fortress fell in 811.⁵ It is perhaps worthy of notice that these operations on the Spanish border appear to correspond chronologically with the arrival of Hārūn's mission, though our authorities give no indication of any connection between them.

The explanation, however, may perhaps be found in the military operations of 'Abdu'l-Raḥmān, the son of Al-Ḥakam, and the policy of Cordova as revealed in the appointment of the renegade Amrūs as *walī* of Toledo in 807.⁶ His commission apparently included Saragossa and Huesca within his *wilāyat*. It would seem that these towns had been lost during 'Abdu'l-Raḥmān's campaign in 808. This reverse mattered little, for on the death of Count Aureolus, the warden of the Spanish Mark, Amrūs took over his property, castles, and charge; substituted his own troops for the garrisons of Aureolus; and in 810 sent an embassy to Charles promising the submission of himself and all his followers to the Frank.⁷ Charles did not reject

¹ *Ibid.*, a. 801; *Vita Hlud. Pii*, no. 47, cc. 10, 13.
² *Vita. Hlud. Pii*, no. 47, c. 13.
³ *Ann. Reg. Franc.*, no. 11, a. 806; Lembke, no. 113, I, 378. The movements which occurred about this time may possibly be connected with the Mālikite conspiracy. See *supra*, p. 18.
⁴ *Ann. Reg. Franc.*, no. 11, a. 806, 809–810; *Vita Hlud. Pii*, no. 47, cc. 14–15. For the date, see Abel and Simson, no. 51, p. 396, n. 3; Lembke, no. 113, I, 379.
⁵ *Vita Hlud. Pii*, no. 47, c. 16.
⁶ Dozy, no. 84, pp. 246–249.
⁷ *Ann. Reg. Franc.*, no. 11, a. 809.

his advances, and in the following year Amrūs sent a fresh mission, repeating his promise of homage and requesting a meeting with Charles's wardens of the frontier with a view to coöperation. Charles apparently agreed to the step, though, owing to the pressure of other business, nothing came of it.[1] Possibly connected with this transaction, or the news of it, is the mission sent by Al-Ḥakam in 810, returning the captured Haimric and requesting peace. This appears to have been agreed to, and, after the fall of Tortosa in 811, confirmed in 812, the year in which Charles was recognized as Emperor by the Byzantine ambassadors.[2] The terms of the treaty are unknown.

Here this chapter of Oriental diplomacy draws to a natural close. Charles was at peace with Constantinople and Cordova. He had, apparently, either in this year or in a previous year made diplomatic representations through Gregory of Sicily against the continuance of Moorish naval raids or piracy—Charles clearly regarded them as authorized and therefore in the former category—and the reply was an authoritative statement that the Khalīfah had handed over to his care the affairs of Spain and the Western Mediterranean.[3] Al-Amīn died in 813 and Charles died in 814. Under their successors began the breakdown of the central power of the Empires which they had inherited before the turbulence of overgrown feudal vassals. One more exchange of diplomatic compliments occurred in 831, when Mā'mūn, on the eve of renewed hostilities with Byzantium, sent two ambassadors, one a Muslim the other a Christian, to Louis. They were favourably received and honourably dismissed.[4]

[1] *Ibid.*, a. 810.
[2] *Ibid.* 'Imperator Aquasgrani veniens mense Octimbrio memoratas legationes audivit, pacemque cum Niciforo imperatore et cum Abulaz rege Hispaniae fecit. Nam . . . et Haimricum comitem olim a Sarracenis captum, Abulaz remittente, recepit.' Cf. Lembke, no. 113, I, 372 f.
[3] Jaffé, no. 26, pp. 325 ff. See *supra*, pp. 24-25.
[4] *Ann. Reg. Franc.*, no. 11, a. 831; Bury, no. 74, pp. 251 ff., 472 ff. Vasiliev (no. 132, p. 79) effectively meets Barthold's contention that this mission was unnecessary, on account of 'Abbāsid victories in 831, by showing that Muslim victories against the Byzantine Empire are not found before July, 831. On Mā'mūn's difficulties in 830, and the attempt on the part of the Emperor Theophilus to embarrass him, see Bury, no. 74, p. 252. Vasiliev (*loc. cit.*) points out significantly that the phrase *confirmatio pacis* implies the existence of peaceful relations atthe time (cf. p. 25, n. 1). The additional fact, quoted by Vasiliev, that Louis rejected the sugges-

In conclusion, the problem of the silence of Muslim historians must be faced.[1] First of all, it should be observed that this silence is not so strange as it would at first sight appear to be, even if complete records had survived. To a resident of Baghdād, the greatness of Charles would be less apparent than it would be to a resident of Rome or York. His state lay beyond the Roman Empire and he would appear to be little more than a barbarian of the extreme West. His very remoteness would be a factor against any record being made, unless curiosity should arouse interest.[2] Secondly, the relations with Charles were occasioned by the affairs of Spain, a dark spot on the horizon, where the early 'Abbāsids' career of victory had been checked by successful resistance. As long as an Umayyad lived and reigned they could not regard their conquests as complete.

In addition, the tactics of employing the infidel against the Faithful was likely to arouse serious antagonism among the stricter Muslimīn, who would regard it not merely as a breach of the law of the Prophet, but also as a dangerous expedient. There is clear evidence of this attitude under Mā'mūn in the proclamation against the employment of Christians and Jews.[3] Thirdly, there are traces of the presence of Franks at the court of the Khalīfah both in the *Thousand and One Nights* and in modern Persian tradition, though it is difficult to disentangle these traces from tales of the Crusades and later trading missions.[4] None of these arguments in itself can be regarded as final, but their cumulative effect has a certain force. It is, indeed,

tion of Theophilus that he should raid 'some Saracen localities and the cities between Lybia and Syria' on the ground of 'his friendship with the Eastern Caliph,' silences more than one objection of Barthold. For later relations, which really form a separate chapter, see Jacob, no. 104.

[1] Barthold appears to regard the silence as evidence that nothing took place. Cf. Joranson, no. 107, pp. 258, n. 75, and 259; Kleinclausz, no. 109, pp. 212–213. See Appendix I.

[2] Cf. the attitude towards kings of the West as late as the sixteenth and seventeenth centuries; there is no mention of Sir Thomas Roe in Jahāngīr's autobiography, even as a matter of curiosity.

[3] Cf. Arnold, *loc. cit. supra*, p. 28, n. 1.

[4] From the nature of the relations involved, the Crusades would not be likely to offer many occasions for the presence of Frankish envoys at Baghdād, and therefore their influence may be set aside. Browne, no. 66, pp. 77–78, gives an instance; allusions occur in the Arabian Nights; 'Alī Ṭabarī, no. 5, p. 133, mentions the Franks among other peoples, distinguishing them from the Greeks. Mas'ūdī makes frequent allusion to the Franks. It also seems probable, therefore, that the term Farangī was in use in Muslim countries before the Crusades.

impossible to build up a negative argument from a silence in authorities presumably hostile to the policy revealed by the events without supplying a definite reason for the inclusion of the events in their narratives. If we possessed the records of the *wāqiʿ a navīs* or court diarist of the 'Abbāsids, it would certainly be there, but its meagre results, in the eyes of an Oriental, would scarcely justify its inclusion in a history of the period. There is one piece of evidence, however, not altogether certain but of some probability, which may have survived, in the form of one of the robes sent by Hārūn to Charles, in the Library of the Dean and Chapter of Durham Cathedral. After the break-up of the Carolingian Empire in 888, it seems probable that its collection of Oriental treasures fell into the hands of the dukes of France, and that in 924, when Duke Hugh wished to obtain the hand of Æthelda, the sister of King Æthelstan, he sent a large part of the collection to the English king. Twelve years later, Æthelstan presented a number of gifts, including seven *pallia*, to the monastery of Saint Cuthbert. In 1104, when the relics of the Saint were disinterred, the monks, in order to provide a worthy shroud, selected a 'pallium quod coeteris pretiosum in ecclesia poterat inveniri.' In 1827 the relics were again disinterred, and there still remained portions of the *pallium*, which answers to the description of a *pallium siricum et preciosum*, and its design appears to be based on the usual conventional representations of the River Tigris. In the design is woven the *kalima*, in Kufic script, *Lā ilāh illā Allāh*.[1]

[1] See Appendix IV. In addition, Barthold gives the following list of surviving gifts from these negotiations (no. 55, p. 80): (1) An ivory horn, preserved at Aachen (Floss, no. 91, pp. 166 f.). Barthold remarks that 'it was this horn which made Charles desire a specimen of the animal whose tooth it was possible thus to shape.' (2) A sword, now in the Vienna Schatzkammer. (3) A golden tray, inlaid with glass of different colours, with the crowned image of Khusrū I in crystal, in the Abbey of Saint-Denis. (4) Eastern chessmen, in the same abbey, according to an eighteenth-century inventory. (5) A golden pitcher, probably given by Charles to the Abbey in Canton Vallis. (6) Eight thorns from the Crown of Thorns, now in Aachen. At the end of the eleventh century, the legend had arisen that Charles had visited Jerusalem and Constantinople and taken these thorns from the Crown of the Saviour (Mély, no. 118). For a list of gifts stated to be taken from the treasury of Charles the Great, see William of Malmesbury, no. 48, I,. 150–151. Reference, too, may be made to Keller, no. 108, for other means by which Oriental wares might find their way to the West and to these regions in particular. An interesting example of a copy of an Arabic *dinār* is found in a gold coin of Offa (757–796) (British Museum, no. 61, pp. 113–114). I am indebted to Mr. Louis G. Clarke, Fellow of Trinity Hall, Cambridge, for this reference.

APPENDIX I

CHARLES THE GREAT AND HARUN AR-RASHID BY W. W. BARTHOLD[1]

THE tales (P. 69) of Frankish chroniclers concerning two possible embassies from Charles the Great to Hārūn and two returning embassies from the Caliph to Charles have been the subject of many investigations, not always happy, owing to their failure to weigh the accuracy of the Frankish sources or to take into account the complete silence of Arabic writers. In the thirties of the last century, Pouqueville concluded that the tales were legends which could have no place in any serious historical work.[2] (P. 70) He did not, however, deny the gift of the Keys of the Holy Sepulchre, the banner of Jerusalem, or the elephant apparently given by the Caliph, though concerning the last, he attributes to the guile of Isaac the story that it was a present from the Caliph. Pouqueville does not mention the embassy of 807.

Pouqueville's vagueness and contradictions gave rise to a total denial of his views by P. Reinaud in 1836,[3] on the grounds that communications between the Franks and the Caliphate occur both before and after the reign of Charles, and that the African Muslimīn continued their attacks on the Frankish Empire in defiance of the Caliph. Reinaud, however, does not cite primary sources, but is contented with Bouquet's *Recueil des historiens de la France*; he does not differentiate between primary historical sources and later legends (e.g., the translation of the relics of St Cyprian); he mentions only in a note the fact that Arabic sources are silent on the question.

(P. 71) From the time of Reinaud to the present (1912) the question has not been reviewed by any Orientalist. Non-Orientalist historians always assume the relations as an undoubted fact, deriving their information from such fantastic sources as *The Thousand and One Nights*, and supposing them to be based on common hatred of

---

[1] No. 55. The article is in Russian, and this summary is made for the use of Occidental readers who are not familiar with that language.
[2] No. 124, pp. 529 ff.
[3] No. 128, pp. 116 ff., 123 ff.

the Umayyad and 'mutual respect.'[1] Therefore a review of the question does not seem to be superfluous.

At the beginning of the ninth century, what interests could the Western European Emperor and his subjects have had in the East, or the Caliph and his subjects in the West? What reliance, in the light of the answers to the above questions, can be placed on the statements of Frankish chroniclers concerning the communications between Charles and Hārūn ar-Rashīd?

What events were taking place at the time, according to Arabic sources? In the light of these events, have we the right to suppose that the Caliph knew about Charles the Great and his Empire and was seeking friendly relations with him?

I. Regarding (P. 72) the first question, Einhard supplies no information concerning the Caliphate, and indicates that Charles's interest in the East was mainly religious, aiming at alleviating the distress of his own subjects and other Christians under infidel rule. There were Franks and Romans to be found in Jerusalem. (P. 73) The visit of the monk in 799 and the gifts of the banner and keys had not the significance they acquired later. Muslim geographers in their description of Jerusalem make scarcely any mention of Christian possessions which remained in the hands of the Orthodox, although Jacobites and Nestorians had greater influence at court. (P. 74) Muslim localities were visited by Charles's subjects, particularly Jews, for trade as well as pilgrimage, and their routes thither are known from European sources. These merchants spoke several languages and traded in slaves, eunuchs, brocades, furs, and other Eastern products, journeying by way of Egypt as far as Arabia, India, and China. (P. 75) There were Jewish traders at both courts; though the evidence for the West is not so clear, still the foreigners at the court of Charles were so numerous as to be a burden. In this respect newcomers from the East had some advantage in being able to satisfy Charles's curiosity. The foregoing statement leads to the conclusion that relations between East and West were defined, (P. 76) first by the interests, permanent and temporary, of pilgrims to, and Christian inhabitants in, the Holy Land, and secondly by the interests of Jewish merchants.

[1] E.g., Bertolini, no. 57, pp. 282 ff.

Appendix I 45

II. (P. 77) After relating the events of 801–802, noticing that there is no mention of the dispatch of the embassy under the year 797, Barthold, conceding the arrival of the elephant, asks the question, 'Under what circumstances could Isaac make his journey to the Caliph and back?' and indicates the gaps in the evidence. He also asks, 'Why did the Caliph trust the elephant and gifts to Isaac and send his own envoys ahead empty-handed?' Einhard's remark that the Caliph sent his only elephant makes us suspect that the story of Isaac's stay at the court of the Caliph has the elements of a 'fishy story.' Again, in 807, the envoys returned home 'after four years' absence,' and arrived in Aachen in the following year. On this occasion Einhard tries to make us believe that the Caliph sent gifts to no one except Charles, whose friendship he valued above that of all other kings. There is no mention of any diplomatic requests on the part of Charles, except *propter elephantem bestiam* in 797. It is difficult, too, to believe that the Caliph's envoys would arrive empty-handed. The story of Isaac is preserved in a Jewish tradition (P. 78) whose source is unknown,[1] in connexion with the dispatch of Rabbi Mahir to Narbonne.

After a list of the Caliph's presents in 807, Barthold continues: (P. 79) Hārūn not only consented to all Charles asked, but consented to the Holy Places being placed under his power ('ut illius potestati ascriberetur'). This arrangement, however, could have been made by the Patriarch with the consent of the local authorities.

(P. 80) With regard to the surviving gifts, (P. 81) J. I. Smirnoff, in a private letter, maintains that, even with substantial proofs, it is possible only to indicate the golden tray of Khusrū as a probable gift from Harun to Charles, and even there documentary evidence is lacking; all the rest are late and of no value.[2]

There remain only the analogies from the reigns of Pippin and Louis in 765(8) and 831. Regarding the former, the name of the Caliph is not even mentioned by the Continuator Fredegarii, while the circumstances of the latter are against its validity. Why Mā' mūn, at the time of his victories in Asia Minor, should feel it necessary to ask the Franks for peace, is incomprehensible. The conclu-

[1] Cassel, no. 80, p. 270.
[2] For Barthold's list of these gifts see *supra*, p. 42, n. 1.

sion of such a treaty had meaning only for North Africa, which was in the power of the Aghlabids. (P. 82) There had been no hostilities between 828 and 831, when a Frankish force disembarked on the shores of Africa and devastated part of the country. Thus, we do not find in the stories of Frankish chroniclers any information about political interests by means of which the exchange of embassies between Caliphs and Frankish Emperors could be explained, and no proofs that the persons appearing before Pippin, Charles, and Louis really had the right to speak in the name of the Caliph.

III. Our knowledge of the reign of Hārūn ar-Rashīd suffers from the halo shed by the *Thousand and One Nights*. Even under the Barmakids, the central government was not fully master of the Empire (P. 83). In 796 Hārūn ar-Rashīd was attacked by the inhabitants of Kūfa, and in 800 he was forced to use troops to obtain the payment of the taxes of Baghdād. About that time he appointed Ibrahīm ibn al-Aghlab as governor of Africa. This fact is significant, as the local Arabs were already recognizing Ibrahīm as their leader when the Caliph decided to appoint him, (P. 84) and the authorities agree that the Caliph neither received revenues from nor exerted any influence over Africa.——Barthold then turns to the question of the elephant, and after ruling out the possibility of obtaining it from Africa, examines the relations of Hārūn with India, including the use of agents to purchase elephants, over and above those sent as tribute (Pp. 84–85). He continues: (P. 86) for the epoch of Hārūn it is hard to believe that he had only one elephant left. Further, had it been sent by the Caliph, it would have arrived with the dignity proper to both kings, for the Caliph had adequate sea power, as his naval victories show. Isaac was probably one of Hārūn's agents to India and received (P. 87) permission to take one elephant to Charles; or he may have received permission from Ibrahīm. No certain proof is available, but this sort of thing could certainly have happened at a later date. With reference to Byzantine affairs, it appears that by 806 the relations between Nicephorus and Hārūn were already restored to friendliness (Pp. 87–90), though in 807 hostilities broke out again (P. 91). The coincidence of the sending of gifts to Nicephorus in 806 and the movements of Isaac raise the question whether it was not the gifts first meant for the Byzantine Emperor

Appendix I

that ultimately reached Charles. The name 'Abdullah' mentioned by the Chroniclers is too common a name for Christians as well as Muslimīn to be of any value.——After a discussion of the relations between the Christians and the Muslimīn (Pp. 92–93), Barthold proceeds to show: that Muslim authors not only do not mention the relations of Charles with the Caliph, but did not even know of the existence of Charles or Italy, not to mention the countries of Western Europe. Ibn Rustī preserves some fantastic data concerning the size of Rome, and Idrīsī states that Rome is ruled by an Emperor called the Pope. In the tenth century (P. 93) Mas'ūdī writes that the possessor of Rome was subject to Constantinople until 951–952, when 'he put on a crown and wore purple and red shoes,' as a consequence of which Constantine the son of Leo 'sent his army upon him.' (P. 94) Rashīd ud-Dīn, writing in 705 A.H. (1305–06 A.D.), mentions Charles in his chapter in the Franks, but his source was clearly European, probably a French monk. He says 'he stopped Muslims in their strife to obtain possession of Frankish territory and brought from Jerusalem into the country of the Romans the crown of the Messiah.' The last words refer, of course, not to Charles's relations with Hārūn but to the legend of his pilgrimage to the Holy Land.

Looking into the data given above, it seems that it gives us the right to come to the following conclusion. There is no foundation for doubt that the subjects of Charles the Great penetrated into the empire of Hārūn ar-Rashīd and the subjects of the Caliph into the empire of Charles, and that in the empire of Charles these business relations appeared as exchange of embassies; but neither in Western European nor in Eastern literature is it possible to find any convincing reasons in favour of the supposition that the Caliph and representatives of Muslim government and society knew about Charles and his empire, that to Charles there were sent from the Caliphate embassies sufficiently dignified for his title, or that the Caliph considered his desires as Emperor. The opinion of Pouqueville, expressed about eighty years ago, that for this view of these relations there is no place in serious historical works, seems to us to be justified.

APPENDIX II

THE CHRONOLOGY OF COSMAS, PATRIARCH OF ALEXANDRIA

THE chronology of the patriarchate of Cosmas has long been a vexed problem, but a solution does not appear to be beyond possibility. The available evidence is contained in the Annals of Eutychius of Alexandria,[1] Theophanes' *Chronographia*, and the Epistle of Paul I to Pippin.[2]

Eutychius notices:[3]

1. His elevation to the Patriarchate of Alexandria as a Melchite 'in the seventh year of the Caliphate of Hishām.'

2. That he 'occupied the see for twenty-eight years and then died.'

3. That through Muslim help he gained control of the Jacobite churches of Alexandria.

4. That 'from the time when the Patriarch George fled from Alexandria to Constantinople in the third year of the caliphate of 'Umar ibnu'l-Khaṭṭāb until the institution of Cosmas in the seventh year of the caliphate of Hishām,' the see of Alexandria was without a Melchite patriarch, namely for the space of ninety-seven years.

5. In the fourth year of the Caliphate of Al-Manṣūr, Balatianus was created Patriarch of Alexandria.[4]

Theophanes states:

1. that he was converted from the Monothelite heresy to orthodoxy in A.M. 6234 (A.D. 734), the second year of Constantine V.[5]

2. that he was present with Theodore of Antioch and Theodore of Jerusalem at the Council which condemned Cosmas of Epiphania at Pentecost in the twenty-third year of Constantine II.

---

[1] For Eutychius see *Encycl. of Islām*, no. 87, *s. v.* Sā'īd ibn Batrik; Brockelmann, no. 63, II, 148–149; no. 18, introductions; also the valuable remarks of J. B. Bury in his edition of Gibbon (no. 94, v, 545).

[2] Jaffé, no. 26, p. 138, also, not by name, in his letter to Constantine II (*ibid.*, p. 153).

[3] No. 18, II, 384–393; Migne, *Patrologia Graeca*, CXI, col. 1126; no. 17, II, 45–46.

[4] No. 18, II, 398–400; Migne, *Patrologia Graeca*, CXI, col. 1125; no. 17, II, 49.

[5] No. 45, I, 416, ll. 13–16.

Appendix II

According to the *Regesta Pontificum*, he wrote a letter to Pope Paul I of Rome (757-767).

Le Quien[1] discussed the chronology at length. Taking A.H. 108 or 111 = 726 or 729 (3 or 7 Hishām) as the basis of his calculation and adding twenty-eight years, he places the death of Cosmas in 754 or 757, and abandons the problem. Pagius places his death between 775 and 780, an avowed conjecture, in order to enable him to be present at the council in 763 to condemn his namesake of Epiphania.

Eutychius, however, has, apparently, not only confused the two capitulations of Alexandria and associated the flight of George with the consequences of the battle of Heliopolis in 640 A.D., but also has confused two different persons. George appears to have been both Patriarch and civil governor (*al-Maqauqīs*) of Alexandria. On the order of ʿAmr he built a bridge over the canal crossing the Qalyūb (10 A.H.). Cyrus was sent out later in the same year from Constantinople, and superseded George (20 A.H.). It was he who, according to Michael Syrus, embarked secretly and fled just before the second capture of Alexandria in 25 A.H. (646 A.D.). This flight took place, therefore, not in the third year of ʿUmar, as Eutychius states, but in the third year of ʿUthmān.[2] So this simple emendation of the text at any rate clears up the chronology of Cosmas, for 646+97 = 743 A.D., the date of Cosmas' accession; 743+28 = 771 A.D., the year of his death; 743 = the second year of Constantine V and so satisfies Theophanes, and it is the last year of Hishām, who died in February, 743. The year 771 A.D. = A.H. 154 is the eighteenth year of Al-Manṣūr instead of the fourth year. This change has the advantage of reducing the patriarchate of 'Balatian,' to which Eutychius assigns without comment the extraordinary length of forty-six years, to the reasonable period of thirty-two years.

The results can be summarized as follows:

Cosmas was elevated to the see of Alexandria, 743; (converted to orthodoxy, 743); present at the Council of Palestine, 763; wrote to Pope Paul I, 763-764.

---

[1] No. 114, II, 457-459.

[2] Caetani, no. 77, IV, 64-105; VII, 103-113. Butler, no. 75, pp. 171 ff., 401-426, 508-526; no. 76, pp. 8-14, 54-83. As Butler points out (no. 76, p. 55) 'جرجيس George and قيروس Cyrus are not very unlike,' and the two may well have been fused into one person.

Paul I's letter to Pippin, 764–765, (Pippin's embassy to Al-Manṣūr, 765).

The death of Cosmas after 28 years as Patriarch, 771. Balatian succeeded to the Patriarchate for 32 years. The death of Balatian in the sixteenth year of the Caliphate of Hārūnu'l-Rashīd and the succession of Eustatius, 802–803.[1]

[1] Eutychius, no. 18, II, 408–411; no. 17, II, 52.

APPENDIX III

PROPTER ELEPHANTEM BESTIAM

BARTHOLD admits that the elephant Abū'l-'Abbās must have arrived at Charles's court, as its death at Lippenheim is recorded in 810 A.D.[1] He asks the questions, therefore, conceding the arrival of the elephant: 'Under what circumstances could Isaac make his journey to the Khalīfah and back?' 'Why did the Khalīfah trust the elephant and gifts to Isaac and send his own envoy ahead with empty hands?' He also proceeds to attack Einhard's statement[2] that the Khalīfah sent to Charles 'his only elephant.' Vasiliev appears to regard the elephant to be the aim of the embassy of 797, and that the future relations arose as a sequel.[3] This appears to be a doubtful contention, but his next point seems to be sound, namely, that it is clear that the envoys of Charles had to ask the Khalīfah for the elephant. He lays stress upon the expressions *roganti*[4] and *'missi eius, quos miserat . . . propter elephantum bestiam'*[5] and *'ab Aaron . . . elefantem expetebant.'*[6] This contention is borne out by the name of the elephant, Abū'l-'Abbās, which marks it down as part of a *khil'at* sent by a member of the house of 'Abbās, a point which rules out the suggestions of Barthold that it was procured by Isaac from India, and brought to Charles by the Khalīfah's permission,[7] an explanation which seems to involve a greater strain on credulity than does the chronicler's version of the story, while even Barthold's version involves the Khalīfah's knowledge of Charles.[8] Vasiliev's contention that elephants were a monopoly of the Khalīfah seems to be at least plausible, and Barthold's evidence is drawn from a description of India which is obviously exaggerated. The fact that it was remarked that 'common people' in India possessed elephants suggests that in

---

[1] No. 55, II, 77.
[2] No. 15, c. 17.
[3] No. 132, p. 80.
[4] Einhard, no. 15, c. 16.
[5] *Chron. Moiss.*, no. 13, a. 802.
[6] *Miracula Sancti Genesii*, no. 37, c. 2.
[7] No. 56, III, 278.
[8] *Ibid.*

the Caliphate they did not. Vasiliev's suggestion that in Africa there were no ships available for transporting elephants is not refuted by the statement that in the Indian Ocean there were such ships,[1] for according to Mas'ūdī[2] elephants in North Africa had entirely disappeared by the seventh century of our era and tame elephants were to be found only in India.[3] Obviously with the disappearance of North African elephants trade in them would cease and facilities for them would vanish from the Mediterranean.

[1] No. 56, III, 279.
[2] No. 31, III, 7 ff.
[4] No. 132, p. 84.

APPENDIX IV

AN EXTRACT FROM 'THE PALLIUM OF SAINT CUTHBERT'[1]

IN the relic of the gorgeous *pallium*, in which the monks wrapped the body of Saint Cuthbert in 1104,[2] there is inwoven a curious inscription which appears to be an Arabic sentence or exclamation,[3] marking its origin to be not merely the East, but the Muslim world. As it does not appear to have been brought by a Crusader,[4] it seems to be worth while to investigate the possible channels by means of which the garment could have arrived at Durham for use in the year 1104.

First, then, the garment itself. The material appears to be a kind of silk brocade, heavily interwoven with gold thread. The material is still produced in Damascus, Baghdād, and the region of 'Irāq.[5]

---

[1] The title of this paper is based upon the descriptions of Simeon of Durham (no. 43, I, 225) '... pallium quod caeteris pretiosius in ecclesia poterat inveniri,' and of Reginald of Durham (c. 42). The term here is used of any flowing robe, and is in no way limited exclusively to the ecclesiastical vestment, even at this date.

[2] 'Secundus vero de incomparandi pallii purpura preciosus.'
Reginaldi Mon. Dun. Libellus, c. 42 (ap. Raine, no. 125, app., p. 5): cf. the account of Simeon of Durham (no. 43, I, 225): '... ad ea quibus ante fuerat involutum ex abundanti pallium quod caeteris pretiosium in ecclesia poterat inveniri et subtilissimam superaddiderunt sidonem'; cf. the account from the Bollandists, anno 1104, quoted and translated by Raine, no. 125, p. 80.

Raine identified the relics as the garment referred to by Reginald (no. 125, p. 197), and reproduced the design of one of the fragments (pl. iv).

[3] I reproduce the pattern with the Arabic transcription immediately underneath. The pattern is worked in the Kufic alphabet.

'There is no God (Allāh) save the One.'

It was first noticed by Professor A. Guillaume and my attention was drawn to it by Professor A. Hamilton Thompson.

For similar formations of letters, see Kühnel, no. 110, pp. 27–28, 190. Two of the illustrations are from work of the ninth and tenth centuries.

[4] I have been unable to trace any evidence of such a visit, nor has it been suggested as a solution to the problem.

[5] The material is called مُقَصَّب , translated by MacNaghten (no. 116, I, 536) 'stuffs in-

The ornamentation is of the kind usually found on the back of the more expensive type of *qaftān* or *qabā'*—flowing robes, with loose sleeves, not unlike the *kimono*.[1] Both are definitely outer garments, ornamented for display, and readily taken off (*khala'a*), consequently the type of garment suitable for a robe of honour (*khil'at*). Now the *qabā'* was the ordinary garment of investiture of *amīrs* and other high officers under the 'Abbāsids.[2] Further, the colour is purple. Now, Procopius of Caesaraea, writing in the sixth century, just before the Muslim conquest of Persia, states that the wearing of purple was a right confined to the Emperor of Rome and the King of Persia.[3] Moreover, it is an established fact that the 'Abbāsid Caliphs took over the ritual and prerogatives of their Sāsānian predecessors, and it would be difficult to avoid the deduction that the wearing of purple was one of the prerogatives retained.[4] Another of the rites taken over was, at least according to the Egyptian historian Maqrīzī, the practice of investiture by means of the *khil'at* or robe of honour. Rightly or wrongly, Maqrīzī dates the practice from the early years of Hārūnu'l-Rashīd.[5] These facts alone indicate Baghdād as the probable home of the man who sent the garment to the West.

But, on closer examination, there are not only traces of Sāsānian art in the relics—as the grape pattern, which bears a marked resemblance to the ornamentation of the palace at Mashīta, the typical

---

terwoven with gold'; similarly E. W. Lane (*Arabian Nights*, London, 1839–41, II, 443). For a fuller discussion see Dozy, no. 83, p. 331, n. 9. One of the most celebrated centres of the industry is the Armenian town Ma'din (معدن), hence the adjective Ma'dini (معدني). Dozy, no. 83, p. 83, n. 2; cf. *ibid.*, p. 355, note, a quotation from Nuwairī's *History of Egypt* (fol. 30 v.).

نخلع على المشار اليه منهم اطلس معدنيا بطرز زركش

'He gave the above-mentioned (their chief) a *khil'at* of a piece of Ma'din satin with brocade edges.'

[1] Garments of this kind have three main names, each with its colloquial variants, the *qaftān*, the *qabā'*, and the *farajiyyat*. For descriptions and uses see Dozy, no. 83, pp. 162 ff., 327 ff., 352 ff., and Lane, no. 111, cap. i.

[2] On the use of robes of honour as means of investiture see *supra*, pp. 33 ff.

[3] Procopius, no. 41 (bk. iii, c. i, sects. 18–23). I am indebted to the late Professor J. B. Bury for this reference. Cf. Judges, viii, 26; Esther, viii, 15; Herodotus, iii, 22; Xenophon, no. 49, bk. i, c. iii, sect. 2.

[4] Browne, no. 65, I, 203 ff.; Palmer, no. 123, pp. 35 ff. Dozy (no. 83, p. 20) quotes a passage from the *Arabian Nights*, 'He put on the garment of anger, that is a red (? purple) garment.'

[5] See *supra*, p. 17 n. 1.

Appendix IV

duck, and the grouping of animals and birds in pairs—but there are also marks of definitely royal symbolism.[1] The fish in the pattern are emblems of sovereignty and appear in countries whose ruling houses derived their authority originally from Persia. Traces are found in modern times, both in the Mughal Empire in India and especially in its most Persianized province, Oudh, where the order of the Fish was regarded as the distinctive mark of a ruling Prince.[2] The orders were three in number, the fish, the peacock's feather, and the *nālkī* (palanquin). Colonel Sleeman, writing in 1844, has preserved an interesting tradition of the origin of this order.

These insignia could be used only by the prince who inherited the sovereignty of the one on whom they had been originally conferred. The order of the Fish, or Mahī Marātib, was first instituted by Khusrū Parvīz, king of Persia, and grandson of the celebrated Naushīrvān the Just. Having been deposed by his general, Bahrām, Khusrū fled for protection to the Greek emperor, Maurice, whose daughter, Shīrīn, he married, and he was sent back to Persia, with an army under the command of Narses, who placed him on the throne of his ancestors in the year A.D. 591. He ascertained from his astrologer, Araz Khushasp, that when he ascended the throne the moon was in the constellation of the Fish, and he gave orders to have two balls made of polished steel, which were to be called Kaukabas (planets), and mounted on long poles. These two planets with a large fish made of gold, upon a third pole in the centre, were ordered to be carried in all royal processions immediately after the king, and before the prime minister. . . . He only who inherits the sovereignty can wear the order. . . .[3]

There appears to be no trace of Sleeman's story in contemporary sources, but the tradition, which was current in Hindustān in the earlier half of the nineteenth century, may quite easily have its

[1] For the 'grape' pattern at Mashīta see Rawlinson, no. 127, p. 597 and plate. On the general characteristics of and relations between Sāsānian and Muslim art, see Arnold, no. 53, pp. 11 ff.; Saladin and Migeon, no. 129, I, 32–33; and Gayet, no. 93, p. 126.

[2] Sir William Foster has very kindly supplied me with the following instance mentioned by Sir Thomas Roe. The incident occurred upon Jahāngīr's leaving Ajmīr in November, 1616. 'At the stayres foote . . . one brought a mighty carp; another a dish of white stuff like starch into which hee putt his finger and touched the fish and so rubd it on his forhead, a ceremony used presaging good fortune.' No. 19, II, 321. Certain definite royal rights over fisheries had been abolished by Akbar (Duperron, no. 86, pp. 289–290).

[3] Sleeman, no. 44, pp. 135 ff. and notes.

origin in the facts it reveals. It emanated from either Delhi or Lucknow, and it is significant that Mughal political tradition and sovereignty were of Persian origin, the model of their political institutions was the state of the 'Abbāsid Caliphs, while theirs in turn was based on the Sāsānian State.[1] The tradition, therefore, may quite easily supplement the story of Procopius, and date from his time.

But the most striking point of contact between the story and the relic under consideration is that it explains the arrangement of the six fishes in the design. They are arranged in three pairs. The top part have their heads pointing outwards and upwards at an angle of about thirty degrees. The bottom pair are horizontal with their heads also pointing outwards. The middle pair face inwards, their heads raised at an angle of about twenty degrees from the horizontal. By tracing lines from the head of the top left-hand fish to the head of the bottom left-hand fish by way of their tails and similarly the right; also by tracing a line from tail to tail of the middle pair, by way of their heads, it will be seen that the conventional sign for the constellation *Pisces* emerges.

If we consider these facts—the restricted use of purple, the traditional origin of the order of the Fish (both connected with sovereignty and its transmission), the Sāsānian style of design and the nature of the fabric,—all dating from the sixth century, together with the Muslim inscription, the origin of the garment is associated with a Muslim capital where Sāsānian influence was paramount, and from the eighth century onwards to 1104, Baghdād alone satisfies these conditions. This deduction is confirmed by the water in the pattern, which indicates flowing water with ducks (in pairs) swimming on it, so a river is represented, presumably the Tigris. Consequently there seems to be little doubt that the robe emanated from the court of the 'Abbāsid Caliphs at Baghdād.

---

[1] See *supra*, pp. 32–33; also Sarkar, no. 130, p. 8, and the writer's 'A New Interpretation of Akbar's "Infallibility" Decree of 1579,' no. 70, pp. 591–608.

BIBLIOGRAPHY

This bibliography lays no claim to completeness, but is provided merely to assist the reader in recognizing books and editions mentioned in the text and notes, where the numbers of the bibliography are used in place of the book titles.

M. G. H. = *Monumenta Germaniae Historica*; SS. = Scriptores.

I. SOURCES

1. Abū'l-Faraj (Bar-Hebraeus). *Chronicon Syriacum.* Latin translation by P. J. Bruns and G. W. Kirsch. Leipzig, 1788.
2. —— *Historia Compendiosa Dynastiarum.* Arabic edition with Latin version, ed. E. Pococke. Oxford, 1663.
3. *Akhbār Majmū'at.* Edited, with Spanish translation, by E. Lafuente y Alcantara. Madrid, 1867.
4. Alcuin. *Epistolae.* Migne, *Patrologia Latina*, CI.
5. 'Alī Ṭabarī. *Kitābu'l-Dīn wa'l-Daulat.* Ed. A. Mingana. Manchester: University Press, 1923.
6. *Annales Fuldenses.* Ed. G. H. Pertz, recog. F. Kurze. Hanover, 1891. (*Scriptores Rerum Germanicarum.*)
7. *Annales Laurissenses Minores. M.G.H.*, SS., I, 112-123.
8. *Annales Mettenses. M.G.H.*, SS., I, 314-336.
9. *Annales Mosellani. M.G.H.*, SS., XVI, 491-499.
10. *Annales Petaviani. M.G.H.*, SS., I, 1-18.
11. *Annales Regni Francorum. Qui dicuntur Annales Laurissenses Maiores et Einhardi.* Ed. G. H. Pertz, rec. F. Kurze. Hanover, 1895. (*Scriptores Rerum Germanicarum.*)
12. Cedrenus, Georgius. *Compendium Historiarum.* Ed. I. Bekker. Bonn, 1838-39. 2 vols. (*Corpus Scriptorum Historiae Byzantinae.*)
13. *Chronicon Moissiacense. M.G.H.*, SS., I, 280-313.
14. *Continuator Fredegarii. M.G.H.*, SS. Rerum Merovingicarum, II, 168-193.
15. Einhard (Eginhard). *Vita Caroli Magni Imperatoris.* Ed. L. Halphen. Paris: Champion, 1923.
16. *Epistolae Merovingici et Karolingici Aevi.* Ed. W. Gundlach. Berlin, 1892. (*M.G.H.*)

17. Eutychius, Patriarch of Alexandria. *Annales.* Arabic text, ed. L. Cheikho, B. Carra de Vaux, H. Zayyat. Beirut: Catholic Press, 1906–09. (*Corpus Scriptorum Christianorum Orientalium.*)
18. — Ed. Edward Pococke and John Selden, with Latin translation. Oxford, 1656. (The Latin translation is reproduced in Migne, *Patrologia Graeca*, LXXXVI.)
19. Foster, Sir W. *The Embassy of Sir Thomas Roe.* London, 1899. (Hakluyt Society.)
20. *Gesta Abbatum Fontanellensium. M.G.H.*, SS., II, 270–301.
21. Ibn-'Adhārī al Murāksī. *Al-Bayāno'l-Mogrib.* Ed., with introduction and notes, by R.P.A. Dozy. Leyden, 1848–51.
22. Ibn el Athirī. *Chronicon.* Ed. C. J. Tornberg. Leyden, 1851–76.
23a. Ibnu'l-Ṭiqṭaqā. *Al-Fakhrī.* Ed. H. Derenbourg. Paris, 1895.
23b. — French Translation by Emile Amar. Paris: Leroux, 1910. (*Archives Marocaines*, XVI.)
24. Idrīsī (Edrîsî). *Description de l'Afrique et de l'Espagne.* Arabic text with translation, ed. R. Dozy and M. J. de Goeje. Leyden, 1866.
25. Isidore Pacensis. *Chronicon.* Migne, *Patrologia Latina*, XCVI.
26. Jaffé, P., ed. *Monumenta Carolina.* Berlin, 1867. (*Bibliotheca Rerum Germanicarum*, IV.)
27. *Kitāb el-Istiqça, li-Akhbār doual el-Maghrib el-Aqça (Histoire du Maroc)*, by Ahmad ben Khaled en-Naciri es-Slaoui. Tr. by A. Graulle and G. S. Colin. Paris: Geuthner, 1923–25. (*Archives Marocaines*, XXX–XXXI.)
28. Leo Grammaticus. *Chronographia.* Ed. I. Bekker. Bonn, 1842. (*Corpus Scriptorum Historiae Byzantinae.*)
29. Al-Makkārī (Aḥmad ibn Moḥammad). *The History of the Mohammedan Dynasties in Spain.* Translated with notes by Pascual de Gayangos. London, 1840. (Royal Asiatic Society, Oriental Translation Fund.)
30. N. Manucci. *Storia do Mogor, or, Mogul India, 1653–1708.* Tr. and ed. by W. Irvine. London: Murray, 1907–08. 4 vols. (*Indian Texts Series.*)
31. Mas'ūdī. *Murūju'l-Dhahab.* Arabic text with French transla-

tion (*Les Prairies d'Or*) by Barbier de Meynard and Pavet de Courteille. Paris, 1861–77. 9 vols.
32. —— *Kitābu'l-Tanbīh, wa'l-Ishrāf*. Ed. M. J. de Goeje. Leyden, 1894. (*Bibliotheca Geographorum Arabicorum*, 8.)
33. —— French translation by B. Carra de Vaux under the title *Le livre de l'avertissement et de la revision*. Paris, 1896.
34. Māwardī. *Al-Aḥkāmu'l-sulṭāniyyah*. (Maverdius, *Constitutiones Politicae*.) Ed. M. Enger. Bonn, 1853.
35. —— French translation by E. Fagnan under the title *Les Statuts Gouvernementaux*. Algiers: Jourdan, 1915.
36. Michael Syrus. *Chronique de Michel le Syrien Patriarche Jacobite d'Antioche (1166–1199)*. Ed. and tr. J. B. Chabot. Paris: Leroux, 1899–1905. 3 vols.
37. *Miracula Sancti Genesii*. *M.G.H.*, SS., xv, 169–172.
38. Monachus Sangallensis. Ed. P. Jaffé, *Monumenta Carolina*, (see no. 26), pp. 628–700. (English translation, A. J. Grant, *Early Lives of Charlemagne*, London, 1907.)
39. F. C. Murgotten. *The Origins of the Islamic State*. An English translation of Al Balādhurī, *Kitāb Futuḥ Al-Buldān*. New York: Columbia University Press, 1924.
40. Poeta Saxo. Ed. P. Jaffé, *Monumenta Carolina* (see no. 26), pp. 542–627.
41. Procopius. *De Aedificiis*. In his *Opera*, ed. J. Haury, III, pt. 2. Leipzig: Teubner, 1913.
42. —— *De Bello Persico*. Ed. H. B. Dewing. New York and London, 1914. (*Loeb Classical Library*.)
43. Simeon of Durham. *Opera*. Ed. T. Arnold. London, 1882–85. 2 vols. (*Rolls Series*.)
44. Sleeman, W. H. *Rambles and Recollections of an Indian Official*. Ed. V. A. Smith. Oxford: University Press, 1915.
45. Theophanes. *Chronographia*. Ed. C. de Boor. Leipzig, 1883–85. 2 vols.
46. Viard, J., ed. *Les Grandes Chroniques de France*. Paris: Champion, 1920 –.
47. *Vita Hludovici Pii*. *M.G.H.*, SS., II, 604–648.
48. William of Malmesbury. *Gesta Regum Anglorum*. Ed. W. Stubbs. London, 1887–89. 2 vols. (*Rolls Series*.)

49. Xenophon. *Cyropaedia.* Ed. Walter Miller. London and New York, 1914. 2 vols. (*Loeb Classical Library.*)
50. Zonaras. *Epitome Historiarum.* Vol. III, ed. T. Büttner-Wobst. Bonn, 1897. (*Corpus Scriptorum Historiae Byzantinae.*)

II. OTHER WORKS

51. Abel, S., and Simson, B. *Jahrbücher des fränkischen Reiches unter Karl dem Grossen.* Leipzig, 1866–83. (*Jahrbücher der deutschen Geschichte.*)
52. Arnold, Sir T. W. *The Preaching of Islam.* 2d ed. London: Constable, 1913.
53. — *Survivals of Sasanian and Manichaean Art in Persian Painting.* Oxford: University Press, 1924.
54. — *The Caliphate.* Oxford: University Press, 1924.
55. Barthold, W. W. 'Charles the Great and Harun ar-Rashid' [in Russian]. *Khristianski Vostok* [*The Christian East*], I (1912), 69–94.
56. — 'The Question of Franco-Muslim Relations' [in Russian]. (A reply to A. A. Vasiliev.) *Khristianski Vostok* [*The Christian East*], III (1914), 263–296.
57. Bertolini, Francesco. *Storia delle dominazioni Germaniche in Italia.* Milan, etc., 1876. (*Storia politica d'Italia,* ed. P. Villari, II.)
58. Bréhier, L. 'Les origines des rapports entre la France et la Syrie. Le protectorat de Charlemagne.' *Congrès français de la Syrie à Marseille,* 1919, fasc. II, 15–39.
59. — *L'Eglise et l'Orient au Moyen Age: Les Croisades.* 4th ed. Paris: Gabalda, 1921.
60. — 'Charlemagne et la Palestine.' *Revue historique,* CLVII (1928), 277–290.
61. British Museum. *Accounts* [etc.], no. 186 (1914).
62. Breysig, T. *Jahrbücher des fränkischen Reiches, 714–741. Die Zeit Karl Martells.* Leipzig, 1869. (*Jahrbücher der deutschen Geschichte.*)
63. Brockelmann, C. *Geschichte der Arabischen Litteratur.* Berlin: Felber, 1902. 2 vols.
64. Brooks, E. W. 'The Byzantines and Arabs in the Time of the

Early Abbasids.' *English Historical Review*, xv (1900), 728–747; xvi (1901), 84–92.
65. Browne, E. G. *A Literary History of Persia.* Cambridge: University Press, 1928. 4 vols.
66. — *A Year among the Persians.* London, 1893. Reprinted, Cambridge: University Press, 1926.
67. Buckler, F. W. 'The Oriental Despot.' *The Anglican Theological Review*, x (1928), 238–249.
68. — 'The Human *Khilʻat*.' *The Near East and India*, xxxiv (1928), 269–270.
69. — 'Two instances of *Khilʻat* in the Bible.' *Journal of Theological Studies*, xxiii (1921), 197–199.
70. — 'A New Interpretation of Akbar's "Infallibility" Decree of 1579.' *Journal of the Royal Asiatic Society*, 1924, pp. 591–608.
71. — 'The Political Theory of the Indian Mutiny.' *Transactions of the Royal Historical Society*, 4th series, v (1923), 71–100.
72. — 'The *Pallium* of Saint Cuthbert.' *Archaeologia Aeliana*, 4th series, I (1925), 199–214. [Appendix IV = pp. 199–204.]
73. Bury, J. B. *A History of the Later Roman Empire from Arcadius to Irene.* London, 1889. 2 vols.
74. — *A History of the Eastern Roman Empire from the Fall of Irene to the Accession of Basil I.* London: Macmillan, 1912.
75. Butler, A. J. *The Arab Conquest of Egypt, and the Last Thirty Years of Roman Dominion.* Oxford: University Press, 1902.
76. — *The Treaty of Miṣr in Ṭabarī.* Oxford: University Press, 1906.
77. Caetani, Leone, Prince of Teano, compiler. *Annali dell'Islām.* Milan: Hoepli, 1905–. 10 vols. issued.
78. *Cambridge Medieval History.* Ed. by H. M. Gwatkin, J. P. Whitney, and others. Cambridge: University Press, 1911 –.
79. Carlyle, Thomas. *The Early Kings of Norway.* London: Chapman and Hall, 1896.
80. Cassel, David. *Lehrbuch der jüdischen Geschichte und Literatur.* Leipzig, 1879.
81. Dahn, F. *Urgeschichte der germanischen und romanischen Völker.* Berlin, 1881–89. 4 vols. (*Allgemeine Geschichte in Einzeldarstellungen.*)

82. Dorr, R. *De Bellis Francorum cum Arabibus gestis usque ad Obitum Karoli Magni.* Königsberg, 1861.
83. Dozy, A. *Dictionnaire détaillé des noms de vêtements chez les Arabes.* Amsterdam, 1845.
84. — *Spanish Islam, a History of the Moslems in Spain.* Tr. by F. G. Stokes. London: Chatto and Windus, 1913.
85. Duff, J. C. Grant. *A History of the Mahrattas.* Ed. S. M. Edwardes. Oxford: University Press, 1921. 2 vols.
86. Duperron, A. H. Anquetil. *Législation orientale.* Amsterdam, 1778.
87. *Encyclopaedia of Islām.* Ed. M. T. Houtsma, A. J. Wensinck, T. W. Arnold, and others. Leyden: Brill, and London: Luzac, 1908– .
88. Fagnan, E. 'Les Tabakāt Malekites.' *Homenaje à Francisco Codera,* pp. 105–113. Saragossa, 1904.
89. Fauriel, M. *Histoire de la Gaule méridionale sous la domination des conquérants germains.* Paris, 1836. 4 vols.
90. Finlay, G. *History of Greece.* Ed. H. F. Tozer. Oxford, 1877. 7 vols.
91. Floss, H. *Geschichtliche Nachrichten über der Aachener Heiligthümer.* Bonn, 1855.
92. Freeman, E. A. *Western Europe in the Eighth Century and Onward.* London: Macmillan, 1904.
93. Gayet, A. *L'art persan.* Paris, 1895.
94. Gibbon, Edward. *The Decline and Fall of the Roman Empire.* Ed. with notes and appendices by J. B. Bury. London: Methuen, 1906. 7 vols.
95. Goldziher, I. *Vorlesungen über den Islam.* 2d ed. Heidelberg: Winter, 1925.
96. — '*Ombre de Dieu, Khalife de Dieu* pour désigner les chefs dans l'Islam.' *Revue de l'histoire des religions,* xxxv (1897), 331–338.
97. Halphen, L. *Etudes critiques sur l'histoire de Charlemagne.* Paris: Félix Alcan, 1921.
98. Harnack, A. *Die Beziehungen des fränkisch-italischen zu dem byzantinischen Reich unter der Regierung Karls des Grossen und der späteren Kaiser karolingischen Stammes.* Göttingen, 1880.

Bibliography

99. — *A History of Dogma*. Tr. by Neil Buchanan et al. London: Williams and Norgate, 1894–99. 7 vols. (*Theological Translation Library*.)
100. Hartmann, L. M. *Geschichte Italiens im Mittelalter*, II. Leipzig: Wigand, 1897–1903.
101. Hartmann, M. 'Die Islamisch-Fränkischen Staatsverträge.' *Zeitschrift für Politik*, XI (1918), 1–64.
102. Hefele, J. *Histoire des Conciles*. Tr. and ed. by H. LeClercq. Vol. III. Paris: Letouzey, 1909.
103. Huart, Clément. *Histoire des Arabes*. Paris: Geuthner, 1912–13. 2 vols.
104. Jacob, G. *Arabische Berichte von Gesandten an germanische Fürstenhöfe aus dem 9. und 10. Jahrhundert*. Berlin: Gruyter, 1927.
105. Jaffé, P., ed. *Regesta pontificum Romanorum ab condita Ecclesia ad Annum p. Chr. MCXCVIII*. 2d ed. by G. Wattenbach. Leipzig, 1885–88. 2 vols.
106. Jamīlu'l-Mudawwar Nakhla. *Haḍāratu'l-Islām fī dāri'l-salām*. Cairo, 1905.
107. Joranson, E. 'The Alleged Frankish Protectorate in Palestine.' *The American Historical Review*, XXXII (1927), 241–261.
108. Keller, F. 'Der Einfall der Sarazenen in die Schweiz.' *Mittheilungen der Antiquarischen Gesellschaft in Zürich*, XI (1856–57), 1–30.
109. Kleinclausz, A. 'La Légende du Protectorat de Charlemagne sur la Terre Sainte.' *Syria*, VII (1926), 211–233.
110. Kühnel, E. *Islamische Kleinkunst*. Berlin: Schmidt, 1925.
111. Lane, E. W. *An Account of the Manners and Customs of the Modern Egyptians*. Everyman edition.
112. Langen, J. *Geschichte der Römischen Kirche von Leo I bis Nikolaus I*. Bonn, 1885.
113. Lembke, F. W., et al. *Geschichte Spaniens*. Hamburg, 1831–1902. 7 vols.
114. Le Quien, M. *Oriens Christianus*. Paris, 1740. 3 vols.
115. MacDonald, D. B. *Muslim Theology, Jurisprudence, and Constitutional Theory*. New York and London: Scribner, 1903.
116. MacNaghten, W. H., ed. *The Alif Laila, or Book of the Thousand Nights and One Night*. Calcutta, 1839–42. 4 vols.

117. Manitius, M. *Geschichte der lateinischen Literatur im Mittelalter.* Munich: C. H. Beck, 1911– .
118. Mély, F. de. 'L'apport de la sainte couronne à Constantinople et la chanson de Charlemagne.' Académie des Inscriptions et Belles-Lettres, *Comptes rendus*, 1899, pp. 590–595.
119. Müller, A. *Der Islam in Morgen- und Abendland.* Berlin, 1885.
120. Muir, Sir William *The Caliphate, its Rise, Decline, and Fall.* Ed. T. H. Weir. Edinburgh: Grant, 1924.
121. Nöldeke, Th. *Sketches from Eastern History.* Tr. by J. S. Black. London, 1892.
122. Oelsner, L. *Jahrbücher des fränkischen Reiches unter König Pippin.* Leipzig, 1871. (*Jahrbücher der deutschen Geschichte.*)
123. Palmer, E. H. *Haroun Alraschid.* London, 1881. (*The New Plutarch Series.*)
124. Pouqueville, F. C. H. L. 'Mémoire historique et diplomatique sur le commerce et les établissemens français au Levant., Institut de France, Académie des Inscriptions et Belles-Lettres, *Mémoires*, x (1833), pp. 513–578.
125. Raine, J. *Saint Cuthbert.* Durham, 1828.
126. Rauschen, G. *Die Legende Karls des Grossen.* Leipzig, 1890.
127. Rawlinson, G. *The Seventh Great Oriental Monarchy.* London, 1876.
128. Reinaud, J. T. *Invasions des Sarrazins en France.* Paris, 1836.
129. Saladin, H., and Migeon, G. *Manuel d'art musulman.* Paris: Picard, 1907. 2 vols.
130. Sarkar, Sir Jadunath. *The Mughal Administration.* [1st series.] Patna: University, 1920.
131. Smith, V. A. *The Early History of India.* 2d ed. Oxford: University Press, 1908.
132. Vasiliev, A. A. 'Karl Veliki i Kharoun-ar-Raschid' [in Russian]. *Vizantiski Vremennik*, xx (1914), 64–116.
133. Wattenbach, W. *Deutschlands Geschichtsquellen.* 6th ed. Berlin, 1893–94. 2 vols.
134. Weil, G. *Geschichte der Chalifen.* Mannheim, 1846–51. 3 vols.
135. Zaydan, J. *Umayyads and 'Abbásids.* Tr. D. S. Margoliouth. Leyden, 1907. (*Gibb Memorial Series*, 4.)